Signs of Agni Yoga
AUM

AUM

1936

Agni Yoga Society
319 West 107th Street
New York NY 10025
www.agniyoga.org

© 1940, 1959 by the Agni Yoga Society.
First edition published 1940. Second edition 1959.

Reprinted 2017. Updated August 2021.
Translated from Russian by the Agni Yoga Society.

ISBN: 978-1-946742-87-2
ISBN (eBook): 978-1-946742-22-3

Entering upon labor, let us beware of weakening in action. Through ignorance it is possible to be filled with thoughts which enfeeble and impede the broadening of consciousness. But let us remind ourselves about the Primary Force. Let us reiterate the principles of the Source of advancement and tirelessness.

The All-bestowing Principle is often forgotten, therefore let us summon all our attentiveness in order to become permeated with the Primary Force.

AUM

1. Let us examine the rainbow—observe that there is in it no blood-red color, nor black; among the higher radiations we find only a radiance and refinement of color. Certain colors which are reminiscent of the higher spheres penetrate to the surface of Earth. Some people love these echoes of the Higher World, but others, on the contrary, prefer the densest shades, and in accordance with such a distinction it is possible to classify people discriminately. One who does not prefer the subtle quality of color has not yet reached a state of ready understanding of the higher worlds. Do not even try to approach such a man, he is under a blood-red cloud. Often such people perish, for their regeneration is almost impossible, and many remedies will fail to benefit them.

2. The physician observes that certain medicines act quite differently on different people. A certain excellent vivifying remedy may act on some people only as an aphrodisiac. People can be tested by their reactions to medicines. A lower nature will draw from substances only the lower, but each entity which is joined to the highest draws precisely the highest. Such a law must be remembered. Even a physician rarely interprets correctly the various effects of medicines. However, there should be commensurateness in everything.

3. Physicians can be true helpers of humanity in the ascent of the spirit. The intellect of a physician must be reinforced by his heart. It should be impossible for the physician to be an ignorant denier. The

physician must be a psychologist, and he must not ignore the wondrous psychic energy. It is not strange that the physician is being mentioned at the beginning of these writings about Aum. All those should be mentioned who are responsible for the bond with the higher energies.

4. If earthly substances act so diversely on different people, then how much more varied is the reaction on them of the highest energies! Long ago people understood that for the proper reception of these rays it is needful to bring the organism into a harmonious condition. For this purpose the Wise Ones have indicated the power of sacred invocations. Aum, or phonetically Om, was such a synthesis of sonant strivings. Prayer and inward concentration are excellent attainments which render healthful the state of the spirit. Each one in his own way has contributed a manifestation useful to spiritual concentration, whether he sought the solution in music, in song, or in the dance; there have even been crude methods leading to intoxication and frenzy. There were many deviations and errors, but fundamentally man was striving to create a particularly exalted state of mind, promoting the reception of the higher energies.

5. A man cannot spend his life without experiencing, though it be but once, the warmth of the heart. Indeed, this will be a fiery sensation, but when it is encircled with a luminous diadem and rainbow, it is then merged with the higher energies. People should not talk and complain that nothing is accessible to them; on the contrary, throughout earthly life they can already sense the great energies. The earthly body cannot always feel such manifestations, it would burn up. But in a lofty state the spirit can nevertheless experience the rays of Grace.

Let people not complain, but live more purely.

6. When you ponder deeply, you will perceive Our path. We are ready to help wherever the law permits. We grieve when We see that people, not having reached the line of salvation, as madmen cast themselves into the abyss. How many thoughts are expended in order to reach the simplest and best result. Yet often the madmen dare to assault the Highest while they are still enveloped by darkness. This is similar to the casting of a stone into the waves of the ocean. True, it may create a little splash, but it can hardly affect the mighty current. Thus it is with all attacks against the great energies. The most savage assault is shattered against the rock of the unconquerable spirit. The boasting of the dark forces only indicates their madness. All-powerful Aum will overcome the most insane and violent attack.

7. At the present time much is being created. In vain may some one think that something does not exist when it is already in existence. Thus it is also with entire nations—some proceed as the dead, others as the newly born. Thus it is in everything.

8. You know well the lightning speed and the suddenness of thoughts sent from Above. The difficulty in remembering such thoughts indicates to what extent an alien energy is intruding into the usual stream of consciousness. Such forgetfulness depends not upon the quality of consciousness, but upon a completely different condition pertaining to powerful energies. It must be noted how difficult it is to retain such sendings in the memory. Ordinary efforts to remember are of no avail; if sendings are recalled, it is in some unexpected way, that is, through contact with a similar energy.

The ancient wisdom taught that for recalling such

sendings it is necessary to press upon the third eye. This counsel was very wise, for by simply pressing the bridge of the nose with the fingers one can cause the center of the third eye to retain the ray of the thought. Likewise, you well know that the state of highest Samadhi is dangerous for the earthly body. The power of the higher energies may not be transmitted through fragile vehicles, yet by overcoming the usual state of disharmony one may render less dangerous the contacts of the higher wings. Again let us recall the various means for bringing oneself into an exalted state. From antiquity people have attempted by special means to shield themselves from danger in contacting the Higher Forces. But the best expedient will be constant thought about the Higher Forces. By such means psychic energy becomes accustomed to the possibility of reaction to the Higher Forces and, in order that it be not shaken, the nerve substance is reinforced accordingly. Of course even one's best friend can cause a shock if he enters unexpectedly.

9. Very few people remain unterrified if told what actually surrounds them. Let us enumerate the rays and all the chemical influences, both from the far-off worlds and from Earth itself. Indeed, reflected and refracted rays differ greatly from the basic ones. When, however, man hears that instead of his being surrounded merely by air in the earthly sense he is surrounded by crystals of granulations and even by continuous explosions, then many hearts become terrified. Of course the air is blue and empty, Earth firm and immovable, and the sun plays the part of a lantern! Ask the shopkeeper on the corner—his conception will be not very far from these beliefs. Only a minority of people attempt to think about their surroundings.

10. Unwillingness to think conceals the entrance

into the future. Meanwhile let us picture to ourselves the difference of consciousness in each century. The difference in qualities of consciousness is amazing. Often the degree of ignorance will be almost identical, but its qualities will be different. These fluctuations must be noted in the history of culture, and a most remarkably steep spiral will become evident. Let us observe how these circles of the spiral have almost touched each other at times, and then receded in order to return upward. Therefore one may be an optimist.

11. I can rejoice when I see the warriors full of vigor. There are many paths and the persecutors will pursue them in vain. Moreover, each battle with darkness is a worthy action. Each dispersion of darkness is the duty of man. The hero calls forth the dragon with a trumpet call in order to slay it. As long as the serpent is underground, people will have no peace at their hearths. Each extermination of evil will be construction of the future. The hero cannot be disheartened.

12. Psychic energy and the transmittance of thoughts from without are manifested widely through creativeness, through research, and through discovery. The sendings may be human ones, or those of the Subtle World or the Fiery World, or finally, those from the ineffable highest spheres. Often it is not easy to distinguish the degree of these transmissions. For this it is necessary to be highly observant of oneself and one's surroundings. Upon alert observation one will succeed in distinguishing certain signs.

Earthly thoughts readily settle into the consciousness, but evil thoughts can provoke a shock to the nerves of an unpleasant nature. Thoughts from the Subtle World will produce a certain heart palpitation and are not so easily assimilated; they may even cause a headache as if the brain were being pierced.

Fiery thoughts flash like meteors, and when a flight of fiery messengers kindles the surrounding atmosphere there results a roaring sound. The manifestation of fiery thoughts is accompanied by fires, and it even intercepts the current of usual thinking. Fiery thoughts are very transitory and are easily forgotten. But the rarely attainable, luminous transmissions of the higher spheres are like lightning, in both their unexpectedness and their penetration of the heart. Only exceptional people can endure these lightnings. One may enumerate many signs of thought sendings, but it is especially important to accept the fact of such transmissions.

13. One should realize in the heart that people are not torn away from the higher worlds. Such a resolute consciousness helps one to recognize one of the greatest wonders—into whatever heights of the stratosphere one may ascend, whatever flights one may contemplate, lofty thought soars freely in every realm. Just reflect that a thought from out the Infinite is carried through all the worlds. Aum is the power of Grace. Already in remote antiquity people realized Divine Omniscience as an all-pervading energy.

Is not then a thought from Infinity a great miracle!

14. The reception of a living thought from out Infinity is in itself an affirmation of man as a spiritualized being, a messenger, a guardian of light. Few understand the wondrous significance of living spatial thought. Will not the world bloom for the consciousness which assimilates the beauty of living thought? I affirm that thought from Infinity flows in a comprehensible form.

15. Spatial thought is sometimes explained as the pressure and fluctuation of thought from the far-off worlds. Thought, being rotated as it were, in the megaphone of Infinity, is purified, and, returns exalted to the manifested worlds. More than once have people tried to advance their own mechanistic explanations, but all such attempts merely demonstrate a limitation of thinking. Through egoism man wishes that his own thought be returned exalted. But when we know the infinitude of Hierarchy, a far more majestic solution will be appropriate. Let us not demean where it is possible to exalt!

16. Thought can move bodies and solid objects. Likewise must spatial thought react. For example one may point to experiments already performed many centuries ago. To the ceiling of the dwelling were attached many threads of different thicknesses and colors, and then, bringing the dwelling into a state of tranquillity, thoughts were sent out. The so-called harp of the spirit began to vibrate, and it could then be noted how certain thoughts affected threads of a definite color; then it was possible to observe the impact of thoughts sent from afar. Of course, during such experiments one should know how to free oneself from one's own involuntary sendings. All may remember how at times slight objects began to vibrate without apparent cause; for skeptics this is merely a draught of air like that in their own heads. The egotism of people makes them reluctant to concede the existence of anything above their own majesty.

17. All manifestations of spatial thought should be remembered. Each one can sense at times something like an invisible cobweb upon his face. It is possible for each one to feel a touch or to turn to a call inaudible to others. Man can hear radio waves without any apparatus, which means that other waves can also be registered by the human receiver. It is very important to observe that sensitivity can even affect a physical wave. Just so is it possible to receive the thoughts of the distant worlds.

18. Do many concern themselves with spatial thought? It is distressing to realize how few. Is it possible to pass one's entire life with never a thought about the Highest? Examples of such vegetative existence are before our eyes. But no one, under any circumstances, should ever place himself on a level with the lowest. Let us recognize what man receives from even one approach to the far-off worlds. Such an approach separates man from all that is low. A single vision of the distant worlds is enough to transform one's entire life. To understand even a particle of life in the other worlds is to acquire a vivid remembrance forever. Such an approach is already an illumination of the consciousness. Aum is the power of Grace, and help is at hand for each one ready to set sail from the shore of the flesh. Even the smallest approaches to spatial thought should be valued.

In place of mistrust and denials, let the chords of the distant worlds resound. Each perception of voices at a distance is already a conquest of space. Some know the music of the spheres and the song of space. Few have approached this step, nevertheless these transfigurers of life do exist. Let us guard such heralds of the far-off worlds.

19. It is essential to understand the meaning of help. Each one wishes to receive help according to his own formula, but not many apprehend true help. Likewise, nowadays when the world is atremble, great numbers of people do not notice the fiery peril. For a special manifestation they want an Archangel as vast as the heavens! Each day something indescribable takes place. Though but a week of the year has passed, consider what has already taken place! Many nations are changing their faces.

20. Leave not Earth derelict. Realization of the distant worlds must broaden one's consciousness, but one must not turn away from earthly suffering. Otherwise everyone will take flight and abandon his hearth. It is necessary to co-measure so that there be no conflict between the heavenly and the earthly.

21. The perfecting of earthly labor will not harm the cognition of the distant worlds. The quality of labor develops also the ability of concentration on all planes. Let us not diminish but multiply our possibilities. He who selflessly desires to succeed can find the path to the higher worlds.

22. A ship succeeds in returning when the sea is calm, but seamen know how storms arise and they plan ahead for unforeseen delays. Thus, in the very best decisions it is possible to foresee elemental difficulties. But there are no frightful outbreaks of chaos where the spirit is striving toward the higher worlds— it soars above the waves of chaos.

23. Each stone on the planet has been created by thought. Each object has been unfolded by the creative power of thought. Each created object should be respected. One must find forbearance toward imperfection, for each creator was at one time imperfect. Each accumulation is the result of labor and of tension. Only in such a realization do we learn to respect creativeness. Beginning with the small let us cognize the great. In order to begin goal-fittingly the sounding of Aum, one should be permeated with a reverence for the greatness of creation.

Thus, the concept of the power of Grace will be a beautiful gift. Only the best striving receives its recompense. The criterion of the best is understood as conformity with the Highest Principle; a cord will be stretched from one thing to another—left untaut the string hangs loose in space.

24. Besides the achievement of outward heroism, there may be a precious achievement which is unseen. In the spirit the achiever attains the highest creativeness and thus becomes an assistant of the Creator. On Earth and above Earth, in the two worlds thought is merged into one comprehensive flow, and such an attainment resounds for the salvation of humanity.

25. Why say Aum, when it is possible to say prayer? In substance they are the same, but because of its antiquity and refinement the sound Aum will be the stronger in its vibration. Let the resonance of the highest concept be pondered deeply. The word itself is vibration; such resonances are needed for the harmony of space.

Great Spiritual Toilers pray not for themselves.

26. People will come and assert that even the highest Teaching does not satisfy them. They still desire something else. Ask them what personal benefit they desire—you will make no mistake by this inquiry. Their dissatisfaction springs too often from a desire for personal gain. Infinity itself has no lure for such hypocrites. They are interested only in an ardent quest of physical delights. They will not linger long near the Teaching; they will depart as soon as they sense the spiritual, not the physical. It is precisely such people who, failing to find pieces of silver, become the most dreadful traitors. Thus, neither the power of Grace nor Aum will affect or illumine them—the coal black heart remains black and is reduced to ashes.

27. You yourselves see how the best hearts suffer from the dark schemes of peoples. For evil creatures, pure unearthly thoughts are but the targets for mockery. It is impossible to express that which saturates the atmosphere around Earth. The thought-forms of the minions of darkness are as countless claws! The symbol of life—the cross—is sundered by them, as an inadmissible means of ascent. Even if this sign forewarns of danger, the servants of darkness direct their efforts toward shattering it. One should not ignore the machinations of evil. One must be wisely aware of reality, the better to value the power of Grace bestowed for salvation.

28. Sorcery is inadmissible, as a crime against humanity. Sorcery must not be regarded as a wrong against one individual. The effects of sorcery are far more heinous—it violates cosmic manifestations and injects confusion in the supermundane strata. Though the sorcerer has failed to smite his enemy, it does not mean that his blow may not have stricken men elsewhere, perhaps in various countries. The vibration of ill will may find itself affirmed in a most unexpected spot. It is impossible to estimate the number of deaths and sicknesses caused by an evil will! Through space these swarms of claws are borne and none may foresee where this poisonous flock will alight. The powerful spirit shields itself against evil sendings, but somewhere a weak man will receive their infection. Such cosmic damage cannot be estimated. Only the power of the sounding of Aum can bring harmony amid the discordant vibrations. Even the power of Grace cannot act in full measure if on its way it must be expended toward the dispersion of evil. It is imperative to warn humanity against all sorcery.

29. No one should scoff at prayer. Even though it be primitive, nevertheless it is an indication of spirituality. It does not become man to revile the worthiest strivings of a brother. Man has no right to sneer at an offering to the Highest. Usually, base people particularly attack the prayers of others. For them, Aum and other prayers are only a source of inadmissible jests. Very often such base consciousness is encountered as the product of uncouth ignorance.

30. Significant features have attached themselves to various beliefs. In antiquity it was required that before praying the priest should bathe and put on clean garments. Now the reverse has come about—luxurious outer garments are displayed, but cleanliness beneath is forgotten. Let us compare such involutions of basic concepts and reflect on the state of spirituality. To a great extent the significance of invoking the Highest has been forgotten. Many books have been written, yet hearts become silent. Thus, it is necessary to remember that you need not luxury of dress, but cleanliness. Let the purity of the path lead to purity of the heart. Prayer cannot rise from a defiled heart.

31. No faith has ever demanded the building of temples. They have arisen gradually, as a manifestation of reverence. The first Principle has always been spiritual and full of directness. Only later has the law of spirit been subordinated to earthly codes. How many of the best wings have been singed by earthly fires! One should surmount all codes in order to fly upwards strivingly. Therefore, let the sacred consonance, Aum, fill the heart with Grace as in the best days of humanity.

32. Often you find a misunderstanding as to what consonance means. Some imagine it as a loud sound, whereas the sound may be inaudible like the heart's tension. For it is the heart that sings; it resounds and fills the entire organism with a special energy. The prayer itself, Aum, may also be in the heart, but it engenders the same radiations as an uttered sound.

One should become accustomed to the heart's expression. One cannot better express his constant striving than in prayer of the heart.

33. Correctly has it been observed that certain mantrams have lost their meaning and retain only their sound. Thus, we see how important is vibration. For this reason much was not written down, but was transmitted orally. Mere letters without sound produce no results. Moreover, the very quality of the voice has a special significance. A deep chest tone can give greater resonance than a high, flat, or nasal one. Thus, not only melody itself but quality of voice is important. I consider that at present the quality of voice is too little valued. Not volume, nor eloquence, but inner magnetism is important—the same is a fundamental requisite in singing. Many voices have been deprived of their natural qualities by methods of vocal training.

34. Prayer will never lack beauty; from near and far it will carry the same powerful mantram. Learn to love the beauty of the sound. The human voice is in itself a miracle. One can see how the voice carries effectively even without words. Everyone has heard choirs at a distance; though the words had been obliterated, yet the magic of the sound lived.

Thus, it is necessary always to remember how many miracles are inherent in man.

35. Prayer is exaltation and ecstasy. Self-seeking prayer is a more modern practice. How can man pray for himself? Does not the Higher Wisdom know what a man needs? Prayer is a conduit to the current of Benefaction. The current flows abundantly, but it is necessary to be united with it. One must find in one's own heart a concordance worthy to meet and welcome the highest and the most sacred treasure. Therefore, each prayer for self is incommensurate. Only when religions became instruments of state were they occupied with customary petitions for a fee. Prayer and payment—how incongruous! For this reason so many people have been repelled by the paid service. The very joy of prayer of exaltation takes flight at the clang of metal.

36. You have heard the prayer of the birds—the little brothers know how to welcome the light. They summon their most rapturous expression before the grandeur of light. Plants reach out toward the light. Only people dream about their stomachs when their spirits should be filled with the grandeur of the Highest. Thus they commit a sacrilege similar to suicide. Noblest hymns have been written, but people recite them without heart tremor, like the clatter of broken crockery.

It is time to turn back to the basic principles, so that even the example of the lesser brothers may call man back to the higher path.

37. Prayer may be likened to a magnet. The action of prayer makes the heart tense and attracts from space the best thoughts; even though such thoughts of the earthly strata may not be Grace itself, nevertheless they are benign. Enrichment by such thoughts imparts new strength, as does a meeting with friends. One should value such friends. One may not encounter them, but they are close at hand. Space itself is filled with them, one has but to send them a good thought. Prayer has a magnetic quality.

38. The antithesis of prayer is profanity. It defiles and disturbs space. It is forbidden to have in the cities factories that produce poisonous gases; yet the consequences of blasphemy and foul speech are far more harmful. People are unwilling to free themselves from the most harmful substance which generates appalling disasters, not to mention the sicknesses caused by disturbances of the atmosphere. More terrifying than any diseases are the destructions of the strata near the planet. How many prayers and good thoughts are required to fill these abysses and ulcers in space! If arid deserts and cyclones are dangerous, the very same danger is courted when humanity ravages the regenerative forces surrounding it. For self-despoiled shells are like decomposing sepulchres.

Guard against profanity!

39. There can be no truce with Satan. Near Satan there is only slavery. To mollify Satan is impossible. Only without fear is it possible to march over him or through him. There is an ancient legend telling how Satan decided to frighten a hermit. He appeared before him in a most terrifying aspect. But the ascetic was filled with a fiery irradiation and charged upon Satan so that he passed through him, burning his way. The fire of the heart is more powerful than any satanic flame. One should be filled with such fire, then all sneers are transformed into searing grimaces. Thus, let us charge upon Satan.

40. Everyone, even in his daily routine, reveals the peculiarities of his nature. A few love especially the deep blue of the mountain peaks, manifesting there the best affirmation of the spirit; others need verdure, and call it the color of hope; a third group lives cramped in the confines of cities and feels content. Different also are the prayers of such people. Little do they understand each other. Therefore, it is necessary to cultivate the consciousness so that it be made tolerant and able to contact the diverse facets of existence.

41. A hermit was once asked how he could dwell in continuous silence. He was much surprised and said, "On the contrary, I am never silent, but converse constantly—so many companions visit me." The hermit had drawn so near to the invisible world that it had become entirely perceptible to him. Prayer became communion, and that world was affirmed in all its magnitude. To such a spirit his own transition into the Subtle World is altogether imperceptible.

Amidst discourses about the Good one may ascend any and all steps. At first, prayer is external, then it issues from the heart, and after that it becomes a communion with Good.

42. An opinion exists that prayer is something apart from daily life, whereas it is the foundation of life. Without a link with the Higher World humanity would be unthinkable, it would be worse than the beasts! Thus, one may regard this bond with the Higher World as the foundation of Be-ness. It matters not in what language the invocation is uttered. Thought has no tongue, yet it is all-pervading.

43. Some devote themselves entirely to prayer, others are able to combine prayer with labor. Let us not weigh which is the more precious; suffice it that prayer and the link with the Higher World do exist and transform life. Do not be astonished if a worker produces a better quality of work by performing it with an invocation of higher Assistance. Be not amazed if the shortest prayer will be the most efficacious.

Thus, let us commune with the Higher World, not by a command but by inclination of the heart. One may transform earthly life only through the bond with the Higher World, otherwise suffering will not diminish; on the contrary, it will lead to ruin. Ignorance must be uprooted, but the best enlightenment is manifested from Above.

44. There are so many dark consciousnesses to be met who fail to discern the need of a link with the

Higher World. Trash abounds, nevertheless guard children from such ignorance. A petrified heart is no longer a heart, but a piece of rubbish.

Therefore, let us find in everything we do a place for communion with the Higher World.

45. Tranquillity of consciousness develops proportionately with the realization of the Higher World. There is no greater joy and beauty than affirmation of the existence of the Higher World. Prayer is the outcome of realization of the living bond with the Higher World. The very concept of such a bond makes a man strong and aspiring.

Let us manifest reverence for everything bearing signs of the Higher World.

46. Is it possible that people do not perceive the whole satanic plot against the Higher World?

47. Man prays for forgiveness, yet fails to alter his manner of living. Man bewails his misfortune, but does not abandon a single habit which brought him into his state of sorrow. Just praying for forgiveness has no meaning if it is not accompanied by reformation of life. It is not sorrow but hypocrisy when the Higher Wisdom is burdened by self-pity. Equally meaningless is enforced prayer. As long as people do not comprehend the significance of the link with the Higher World, they only blaspheme by the insincerity of their prayers. One cannot lie before Truth, nor conceal anything in the face of all-pervading Light. Moreover, why conceal that which is sacred and justified by the heart? The bond with the Higher World will be attractive when the heart affirms its own judgment.

48. Good and evil are tested by the heart. Thus it is possible to bring to the Highest an unshakable affirmation. One may recognize all relative imperfections, yet be able nonetheless to affirm unhesitatingly the Good.

People try to test criminals by their blood pressure, yet fail to see that a single suspicion in itself may excite the entire organism. It is better to commune with the Higher World, where all the secret scrolls are revealed.

49. Dreams are beyond time; they demonstrate the relativity of earthly measures. Thought also can reach the higher worlds without requiring time. The speediest air mail nevertheless needs time. Let the speed of thought be studied, such observation is useful for realization of the far-off worlds.

50. A sound may be rightly understood and still produce no results. Therefore, let us not forget the heart's energy, which must accompany the sound. It would be unfit if sound alone held the decisive significance; then many singers could attain results. An empty sound is like the clash of brass. You have heard how glass vessels have been shattered by vibration; yet even such vibration must be accompanied by thought. Even a wave of extraneous thought can increase the effect. Therefore, thought as the impelling force is so valued.

One should not be surprised if, in speaking of prayer, emphasis is put on the need of mindfulness of the vibratory conditions. Such investigation of all the attributes of communion with the Higher World will be the true path. The heart should not be forgotten amidst observations, for all the other aspects must be subordinated to the heart.

51. Besides the heart, keep the consciousness clear. It is impossible to see through turbid waters. All agitation will react in a completely identical manner, in water and in the consciousness. One must find the happy medium between responsiveness and excitability. Under earthly conditions it is not easy to avoid excitement, which is so pernicious for good health.

Manifestation of the link with the Higher World bestows a quality of sensitiveness and clarity which is not made turbid by the dark currents.

52. Unity and victory are the best mantram. The strength of the dark ones is shattered against such a rock. One should also remember not to burden the Teacher purposelessly. Let love and devotion also live in the heart.

53. Various rituals which accompany prayers represent futile efforts to intensify the significance of the prayer. For many ages people trained themselves in affirming the importance of the Higher World. But now again humanity has turned away from acceptance of the basic laws. Instead of rituals, science approaches the right path, but in the vanity of worldly life the calls of science remain solitary manifestations.

For these reasons one should again confirm the existence of the Higher World. Shame upon humanity, that it has broken away from the shore of knowledge!

54. The new is regarded as old, therefore the new is forgotten. It should be cleansed, otherwise instead of beautiful Images there will remain only dust-covered masks.

Let us summon every one who is capable of approaching the Great Images without blasphemy. Let him adorn Them according to the custom of his country, for We shall meet the approaching ones on all paths leading to the Higher World.

55. People know that each one sees objects in his own light. Already there are explanations about different eye structures, but they completely fail to add the significant fact that people see through their own aura. Each one has around him his own color through which he sees. Tell physicians this truth and they will ridicule it, because the color of radiations is invisible

and is not mentioned in textbooks of ophthalmology. Yet blindness can result from shock. Thus, also deafness and impairment of the other senses are contingent upon the heart. The radiation itself depends upon the condition of the heart. This means that everything emanating from the heart as prayer is highly polychromic. Let us guard against blood-red and black prayer.

56. Prayer usually evokes azure and violet flame. There may be a silvery prayer, but it is impossible to imagine a brown prayer. The principle of light in earthly existence is highly essential. One may disguise the tone of the voice, but the radiation of the heart cannot be falsified.

57. Prayer is a purifier. This definition should not be understood abstractly. Spiritual health is the primary basis of bodily health. Precisely prayer as a real link with the higher Source will be the best purifier of the organism against all diseases. Infection appears when the body permits the entrance of manifested messengers of evil. Each body is predisposed to many diseases, but spiritual strength is on guard to quell such uprisings. When the spirit can be properly nourished by the higher energies, it also protects the body against dangers.

Therefore, it can be affirmed that prayer is a purifier.

58. There are ignorant ones who assume that prayer is generally out of place in practical life. They should be asked what sort of business they consider incompatible with prayer—that which is evil and greedy? Certainly in evil there is no place for prayer, yet every good work is in need of prayer—that which reveals the Higher Forces.

Thus, in the New World one should affirm the true realities. We shall not retrogress if we keep in mind that which permanently and unalterably will be the law of Existence.

59. One can see what unworthy methods are combined with prayer! Frenzies can be of no assistance toward the link with the Higher World. Eye-witnesses of higher visions affirm that they cannot even remain firm on their feet because of the powerful vibrations. Moreover, visions are preceded by a special serenity of the spirit. Can spinning and whirling possibly be the threshold of a beautiful vision? Man, by his own will, cannot compel a manifestation of the Higher World. It is possible to attract the Subtle World, but the grandeur of the Higher World transcends all earthly nature. For years hermits await the Higher Word. Even great Spiritual Toilers could withstand a manifestation of the Higher World only once without shock to their health. However, the Higher World knows when and what is possible.

60. Reverence of Hierarchy will affirm the closeness of the Higher World. In cooperation with Hierarchy do you find firm bridges to that shore. Every belief reveals the Guardian Angels, Guides, and Comforters; under the various names lies the same concept of Hierarchy. Verily, let each one understand in his own way, but let each heart strive upwards. In this alone is the path to perfection.

The manifestation of prayer is communion with the most Beautiful.

61. Prayer is an inspirer to knowledge. Each one who realizes the sublimity of communion will inevitably begin to strive toward knowledge. The growth of such consciousness requires the accumulation of knowledge in various fields of science. Philosophy discloses the same paths to the Higher World as are disclosed by the natural sciences. Ignorant persons prattle about materialistic sciences which deny everything not visible to the naked eye. Yet they already know about the subtlety of atoms, and they understand the need for microscope and telescope. In truth, they make of science an empty shell. When signs of the Higher World are manifested in the consciousness, then every science becomes transfigured. No knowledge exists which, if truly known, would not confirm the great bond between the worlds. No paths exist which, if truly followed, would not lead to the Higher World. He who does not feel the greatness of Unity and Infinity has not grown in his consciousness. Prayer is not a deathly cry of terror but a communion full of love and devotion.

62. If someone maintains within himself a dull negation without any mental construction, such poverty of thought must be looked upon as madness. How many times have you yourselves encountered such madmen! They arouse nothing but pity. As a small shopkeeper calculates the amount of his profit but ridicules higher mathematics, so does the ignoramus make out of a thorn from the crown of great achievement a toothpick for himself.

Not only does knowledge lead to the Higher World, but labor also. Indeed, each labor is knowledge. Thus, labor is prayer.

63. Through prayer healings are often accomplished. It is not difficult to understand that the bond with the Higher World aids the heart, and carries along the nerves a salutary Benefaction. It is not difficult to understand this even from the conventional scientific viewpoint. The prevalence of ignorance is such that it is necessary to reiterate even this simple consideration, for not a single opportunity of reminding about the

Higher World must be overlooked. Thus, still another prayer is created.

64. It is frightful to see the spectacle of madness when evil attempts to wipe everything rational off the face of Earth. Malice acts like a destructive whirlwind. Only the bond with the Higher World can restore balance.

65. It is especially revolting to see on the one side the utmost devotion to the Higher World, but on the other—dark satanism in full measure. Thus in examples from life it is possible to find the likeness of Armageddon. It must be remembered that the Forces of Light unceasingly smite the darkness. Prayer will be also a battle cry when falsehood is vanquished in the name of the Highest. By dispelling falsehood we serve the Light.

66. Irritation has no kinship with prayer. The defeat of falsehood must take place by the raising of the Fiery Sword, but not through irritation.

67. Prayer does not abase—it exalts. If, after prayer one feels depressed, it means that the quality of prayer was not lofty. A man is not comparable to Infinity, but one spark of higher energy maintains in itself a significance even beyond conceivable boundaries. A spark of higher energy has been given to each man, and as its bearer he is invested with a lofty duty. He is a bridge to the Higher Worlds. Thus in denying the Higher World, the ignoramus repudiates his own humanity.

A reminder about the Higher World is a touchstone for the testing of each spirit.

68. The spiritual principle precedes each action. There can be no bodily action without an antecedent spiritual fusion. Thus, whoever denies the spiritual principle thereby divests his actions of meaning. Evolution cannot continue if the primary motive force is repudiated. The Dark Age has among its characteristics the denial of principles and fundamentals. Yet precisely such darkness is transitory. Man must prepare himself for the acceptance of Light, and, lest he become like a mole, he must realize within himself the essence of Light.

When I speak about the highest communion, I first of all propose that you understand reality in all its infinitude.

69. Prayer has no kinship with violence nor constraint. The first prayer of the child should not be ridiculed or reproved. A boy once prayed, "O Lord, we are ready to help Thee." A passer-by was indignant and called the child presumptuous, and in this way the first feeling of unselfishness was defamed. A little girl prayed about her mother and her cow, and her prayer was ridiculed. Thus her memory retained only something ludicrous, whereas such solicitude was really touching.

Likewise, using the name of God for intimidation is a great blasphemy. Forbiddance to pray in one's own words is in itself an intrusion into the young consciousness. Perhaps the child remembers something very important and extends his thought upward. Who, then, can intrude to smother such a luminous impulse? The first instruction about prayer will be a directive upon the whole path of life.

70. The surroundings at home likewise impose an imprint on one's whole life. Even the poorest hut would not outrage the spiritual feeling. It should not be presumed that futility of life is not noticed by children, on the contrary, they feel keenly the structure of all their everyday life; therefore, prayer lives best in a clean home.

71. Prayer is good at any time, yet there are two

periods of change of currents when turning to the Higher World is especially desirable—at sunrise and after sunset. Besides, upon going to sleep it is befitting to invoke the Higher World.

Sleep is not understood by science. The idea of rest is primitive. If each action is preceded by a spiritual act, then such an extraordinary state as that of sleep must be especially noted. For almost half their lives people entrust themselves to an invisible world. It is necessary to purify one's consciousness before entrance into the sacred Gates. Thought about the Higher World, thought about the Guardians, already lights up the drooping consciousness; hence, there may be more desirable meetings, and attacks may be warded off. Only the heart's thought about the Higher World provides an impenetrable armor.

Thus, let us be conscious of all that is most beautiful and needed on the lengthy journey.

72. Let the heart by its beat always remind one about spiritual food. Lose not the custom of prayer, banish not the good thoughts. Often man deprives himself of the right of entrance. The Higher World is not a consuming fire for friends and co-workers. In life people guard themselves against burns, let them likewise be definitely mindful about their future.

73. It is well to assemble for the unifying of thought; thus you create a spatial beneficence. Such thought is prayer—you do not think of self, you gather together for the Good. Assistance to friends is so far removed from covetousness.

I consider those hours worthiest which are spent in sending thoughts to friends and to all who are in need.

74. With whom may one fortify one's thoughts? Only with the Guru. He is as a rock, near which it is possible to be sheltered from the storm. Reverence for

the Guru is the path to the Higher World. But chaos cannot tolerate construction. One should direct attention to the basis of thought in order not to be exposed to the whirlwind.

75. There are people who aver that they never pray, and yet they preserve an exalted state of mind. The causes are many. It may be that they commune with the Higher World while at work without being aware of this fact. Perhaps their consciousness preserves in the depths of the heart flaming invocations, inaudible to man. It may be that from former lives hieroglyphics in strange languages have been carried over in secret memory. Thus, people often begin to repeat an unknown word which has a meaning in an unexpected dialect. Many sacred remembrances are preserved in the consciousness. Many of the worthiest actions are impelled by causes from former lives. One need not bind oneself by affirmations which have causes deriving from deep experiences.

76. No one bears another's thought. One's judgment will be his own responsibility before the world. One anchorite prayed merely by repeating in his language—Thou, Thou, Thou! He asserted that in the briefest affirmation he concentrated the strongest power. Though tongues may differ, yet consciousnesses aspire to the same goal.

77. The ignorant skeptic asks, "Why make assumptions about some sort of higher worlds? I have never heard of anything of that kind." It is fitting to answer, "Certain kinds of animals do not know about the higher worlds, nevertheless people have seen and felt the higher contacts a great number of times and can speak about their reality. If someone has never once felt the approach of the invisible world, it means that

one's nerve centers have become atrophied." This is the fitting answer to ignorant skepticism.

What kind of prayer is possible in the mouth of a denier? It is impossible even to speak about prayer in the presence of ignorance. The fruit of humiliating attempts will be very bitter. The sensitiveness of the developed consciousness will whisper when it is impossible to refer to the higher worlds.

78. With the utmost reverence, some affirm—"Not That, not That," so as not to admit offensive comparisons. Others altogether forbid pronouncing the word God in order not to belittle the grandeur of the Highest. Thus do people approach Infinity differently. In the depths of their consciousness they feel that it is impossible to express or appraise that which is higher than all possible concepts. A blind man feels the stones of the lower levels, but knows not the height of the tower. Yet man cannot tear himself away from the Ladder of Hierarchy. The traveler will reach the steps of his ascent.

The path of Light sings, and boundless spaces resound!

79. Aum resounds not as a name but as a concept. The cognizing one will realize the sounding which is consonant with the music of the spheres. Rarely is it possible to hear this resonance of the spheres with the earthly ear, but the ignoramus takes it only for a noise in the ear. Thus let us walk there where sounds Infinity itself.

80. Great Love is laid in the foundation of the Higher World. Only a similar love responds to this quality. The most manifested reverence will not reach its destination without love. What is devotion without love? Can there be fieriness in a withered heart? Following a manifestation of love, there can be expected

commensurateness with the Higher World. Each subject can be studied only with love. Each difficulty can be conquered by the power of love.

Verily, great Love lies in the foundation of the Higher World!

81. Great Service can be the lot of every man. New life is poured into him who dares to toil in Great Service. The measures of his entrance will be determined by each one himself. Each one may pledge himself, not to small but to Great Service, and thus irrevocably dedicate himself to the Higher World.

Thus Great Service is a duty and an honor.

82. He who knows how to discern the presence of the Higher World in the smallest things is already on the path of ascent. Indeed, it is needful in everything to link oneself to the Higher World. Without such attachment, the path will be a long one. Amid the densest of earthly conditions it is still possible to direct oneself toward the Higher World, and this World of Beauty will be close by. In the earthly body the spirit already learns to merge into the Higher World as if returning into its own wondrous native realm. Man feels an attraction even to his earthly native land which is transitory; so much the greater is his attraction to the eternal Fatherland. Only chaos can conceal from man the treasure which rightfully belongs to him. The sounding of harmony conquers the confusion of chaos. Aum!

83. Miracles cannot be something abstract for the spirit that is united with the Higher World. Every unusual earthly manifestation is a particle of the very Highest World, in other words, of reality. The same harmonious sounding already reveals the secret entrances. However, observe the smallest signs of the

Higher World. From such small seeds will grow forth the most steadfast tree and the loftiest.

All signs must be attentively watched. Do not overlook those larger manifestations which you may consider, in the delusion of the flesh, unworthy of attention. The flesh is crude, and only the heart beats in the name of the Higher World. Aum!

84. The Fire or Light of the Higher World is not an entirely unusual manifestation. Far oftener than it is thought do these sparks penetrate the earthly strata. Indeed, they are explained as electrical manifestations. Their substance does not differ essentially from that which it has been agreed to call electricity, but such sendings emanate from the thought energy of the Higher World. Not by accident do such fires and lights flash out; either encouragement or forewarning or confirmation resound in these sendings of Light. People usually complain that these messengers arrive unexpectedly. Amidst one's daily labor there may suddenly be seen a luminous indication. Perhaps it may instill courage and vigor and remind one about the Higher World, in order to fix in the masonry of consciousness still another strong stone.

Wondrous are the fires and lights of the Higher World. They do not singe where there is good. Each time they impel one to reflect about that invisible magnitude. One should accept these bridges as the sole path. It is terrible to be afraid of the Light as then Fire turns into a devouring flame. Fear is unfitting, and terror is self-destructive.

85. Convincingness implies trust. Therefore, realization of the Higher World will not be forgotten in many lives. Precisely such a quality remains unalterable forever. So much the more is it necessary to be

affirmed in knowledge of the Higher World. Confirmation will not be delayed in coming.

86. Throughout the history of humanity can be traced a recognition of the Higher Spirit, the Holy Spirit, the Comforter, and a great number of such concepts leading to the Higher World. Such testimony of all ages and peoples must compel even the ignorant to reflect. All mankind cannot be mistaken! Under varying conditions people have sensed the same supreme, ineffable Origin. People have regarded the manifestation of the spirit as the philosophers' stone. One can find the most multiform signs of great Reality preserved by peoples. This is not self-interested suggestion, but a discernment of truth. Let people search in ancient Egypt, in Babylon, amid the undiscovered cultures of the Mayans; and everywhere, beyond the subtle symbols, can be found the same exalted concepts.

Thus science may lead to the Higher World.

87. Lenience is one of the qualities of the Higher World, therefore each one in turn must show this quality wherever there is a spark of good. Let people not weary of seeking this power of Grace. Thus in eternal vigil one may take upon oneself the service of the Higher World. One must not pride oneself on such distinction; no particular pride is fitting, but a special joy is permitted.

88. The bond with the Higher World enriches the consciousness bountifully. In manifold ways do the lofty sendings reach their mark—they may be apprehended in sleep, they may be received in wakefulness as a lightning flash of thought. One should not grieve if such thoughts sometimes seem to be immediately forgotten, rather, they have sunk into the consciousness. It may be that the thought was destined for the innermost consciousness. Only in due time will it be

manifested; meanwhile it must live on and enrich the consciousness.

It is said that growth of the consciousness is similar to the growth of a blade of grass. Man cannot notice the growth of grass by the hour, and just as imperceptibly appears a budding blossom. Only by periods is it possible to observe changes of consciousness; such a change will be indescribable. Consciousness grows by synthesis, it cannot move forward in a narrow manner. Advancement of the consciousness will proceed from the center encompassing successive circles of new understanding.

Likewise, sendings to scientists will not be materially narrow; they will impel the thought toward an expanding horizon. The mind will act as a scabbard for the flaming sword. Thus, tasks with a broad range are presented from the Higher World. Earthly limitations reduce supermundane thought to the human word, yet in the depths of the consciousness is preserved the imprint of the heavenly hieroglyph.

89. It is useful to consider communion with the Higher World to be as necessary as pure air. One need not sit in a fetid, poisonous atmosphere. Even the most ignorant people understand that poison is harmful.

Likewise it may be observed that through spiritual development people free themselves from the unpleasant odors which are natural to undeveloped organisms. Let us realize that the Higher World can transform even the composition of the blood. Let us not think that such reactions are supernatural, on the contrary, they are most natural. When a man returns from the pure outdoor air he emits a fragrant odor. Equally fragrant is the consciousness over-shadowed by Grace.

90. Even earthly thought can move solid objects—

hence one can imagine the scope of the creative power of thought of the Higher World. People say that the conflict of thoughts results in truth, and thus people themselves unsuspectingly affirm a great truth. Truly, the creative power of thought energy is that secret about which sages deliberate. Precisely, not one thought, but the intersection of thought currents forms a spiral of conception. One may adduce many scientific experiments, but first of all it is necessary to establish the physical force of thought. If light objects can be moved under the force of thought, then this can be imagined as a progression in infinity. Not a spiritual nor an ethical calculation, but a physical one can present a concept of the higher magnitude. People should understand that their energy can produce enormous results. The potential of thought has been entrusted to each one and can be utilized scientifically, rationally, or wastefully to the harm of all that exists. Thus, prayer can be a great scientific experiment and proof.

When I say, "Aum," I have in mind benefit to the world.

91. It should not be considered that true science cannot be mentioned in connection with prayer about the Highest Good. Each realization can be very close to the Higher World, yet each one can apply his own observation, and at opposite ends of the world mental currents may be received which by their intersection can create a vortex of new possibilities. Surely, the Higher World is the most beautiful possibility.

92. Broad is the domain of humanity; at its summit it touches the Higher World in the person of heroes, of great Spiritual Toilers; at its base it produces a cosmic dust which forms the stones of the neighboring planets. Enormous is the distance between a great Spiritual

Toiler already illumined by the Light of the Higher World, and the dusty dregs.

In view of the fact that a potential of basic energy has been given to each man, it is difficult to conceive how contrarily people have dealt with this great gift. The very imagination can hardly encompass such a chasm. People regard that which is unpleasant to them as difficult and that which causes them no trouble as easy; out of such conventionality open up yawning abysses. People are not accustomed to keeping the Higher World in their consciousness, yet it is not difficult to replace the feeling of emptiness with infinite life. How much more beautiful is realization of the Higher World than the casting of oneself into stony fetters!

Why begin all over again when it is possible to ascend infinitely?

93. Any feeling can be cultivated. Fearlessness too can be developed. One can set oneself tasks of fearlessness instead of imbuing oneself with a feeling of terror.

Apparitions are just as real as the shadows on the sand, but we know what causes the shadow. So, too, appearances out of the Subtle World will not be an impossibility. But let us not fear; let us resonantly pronounce the Name of the Teacher.

94. There is much fire, and consequently one can understand the waves which burn and fatigue. Subterranean and superterrestrial fires are related, yet they are far apart in their effects. Men are unwilling to understand their own influence upon subterranean fire. Astrological signs suggest thoughts of special caution, but instead men only increase the danger. Of what concern is it to the bipeds, if because of them on another continent a destructive flame bursts out!

95. The law of Cosmos is adamant, but at the same

time we see apparent fluctuations of it. If we take karma, affirmation of karma too can be changed, just as the span between returns to carnate life may vary in different cases—from an instant to millennia. Those who do not know will be perplexed as to how such steadfastness can be at the same time so variable. Such ignorance will merely prove the lack of understanding of containment.

People also fail to understand which energy serves as the deciding factor. In all the cosmic amplitudes the basic factor is thought; it can alter karma, it can determine dates, it opens gates, and it can close them. It grows wing-rays from the shoulders. It can lead one close to the Higher World or precipitate one into the abyss. The manifestation of law rests on thought. The great wisdom of thought is a shield and a guard against chaos. Thought actually rules over the fury of chaos.

Truly, the law of Cosmos is immutable, but it is illumined by thought and therefore goal-fitting. Understanding of co-measurement only teaches comprehension of the fundamental law.

Thus, let us always remember creative thought. Aum!

96. Alteration of karma appears unthinkable to many, but they err, forgetting about heavenly Justice. It is possible to experience instantaneously the highest realizations. Where the foot can tread, there thought can fly. In certain cults the neophytes were plunged into sleep and through hypnotic suggestion were compelled to experience at great speed the entire difficult pathway of their karmic life-pattern. Thus was inevitability understood, and also the possible acceleration of the law. Thought creates life.

97. Not only is it difficult to assimilate the law of karma, it is still more difficult to perceive the elementary law of incarnation. Yet the scriptures of the most ancient times often spoke of such a change of life. Often have the dwellers of the Subtle World communicated to earthly people their tidings. Frequently people remember about their former lives. For whole ages reincarnations have been acknowledged, but later they were again forgotten and it was even forbidden to think about them. It is difficult to comprehend the reason for such a struggle against the evidence. Sometimes it would have seemed that the wise ones wished to turn their attention only to the future, but such wisdom would be one-sided.

People should aspire to unlimited knowledge. One should not command a man not to know. A man should not be deprived of his right to self-perfectment. Let it be known and remembered that the Teacher of life draws a line between past and future.

Thus, let us not close our eyes to reality. The law of incarnation is just. The kernel of the spirit is inviolable and eternal. Infinity affirms Eternity, but everyone can visualize Infinity—which means everyone can realize Eternity.

One should not deny the statements of children about their past lives. Essentially they know what has taken place around them. Especially nowadays there often will be rapid reincarnations. Many dwellers of the Subtle World are hastening to return, and herein is expressed the growth and acceleration of evolution. And in such quickening may be seen a rapprochement between the worlds.

98. Much is needed to convince people that they should observe the principal moments as they occur in their lives. People are so unable to discriminate between the significant and the negligible. Even the key milestones of existence often pass by without drawing attention. The school should be an aid to such enlightenment.

99. It is especially difficult for people to discern what is most important in themselves. If a physician locates a malignant internal tumor, he hastens to cut through the external layers so as to forestall the danger, but the coward will want to spare his skin and will perish from the continued growth of the tumor. If it is necessary to choose, let the most essential be preserved. Similarly, in turning to the Higher World, time must be found for reflecting on the most important.

100. A triple palimpsest provides an example of the stratifications of signs of the three worlds. Let us imagine a parchment on which first was written a cosmogonic treatise, and which later served for a love sonnet, while finally there has been written on it a reckoning of fabrics and furs. Through the obvious bazaar figures it will be difficult to make out the effusions of the heart, and it will be almost impossible to decipher the treatise about the most important. Does not the same thing take place in regard to the hieroglyph of the three worlds? Yet just as the experienced savant is able to read the most complicated manuscripts, an enlightened consciousness can understand the meaning of inscriptions of the Higher World.

Let us not take the jumbled figures of the bazaar for the laws of the Universe.

101. All comparisons are applicable in encounters with ignorance. Deniers like to refute, but they will offer no issue or solution. They ridicule the very best communion, but are unable to connect even three letters.

102. People become pious as they near the crossing into the Subtle World. They fail to discern that such a hurried bribery borders upon blasphemy. Thus there results, not a realization of the Higher World, but a hurried payment for the best place, whereas approach to the Higher World should begin in the first days of earthly life.

Not conventional rites but prayer of the heart brings the World of Beauty near and makes it a daily sustenance. One can approach the Highest with the Chalice filled with the best thoughts. One can offer the best experiments by warranting them to be directed to Good. When the Good lives, it opens all the gates to the Higher World.

103. People, even those who know about the Subtle World, deem it possible to postpone perfecting their thinking until the time comes to enter that world. They are wrong, it is precisely here that the direction of thought must be established. It can be developed once a definite impulse has been given. The test of thinking must be affirmed by earthly thinking. It is deplorable to enter the Subtle World in a confused and distracted state. When the consciousness is clear it leads upward just as gas lifts a balloon. No one and nothing can detain in the lower strata a steadfast consciousness which strives toward Good; therefore let us not defer affirmation of thinking. There is no more direct communion with the Higher World than by this path.

104. Meditation in quiet about the Higher World will be equal to the best remedy. It is possible thus to sense the relativity of that which exists. Such a measure will not be a limitation, on the contrary it will strengthen the flight of thought. When confusion takes possession of the world, propound the most simple.

Earthly existence cannot be final, and in such a transitory state one may only prepare that which is most needed for the future flight, in other words—sharpen thought. Wings grow only through thought.

105. Undoubtedly you are often asked about the contact of the Subtle World with earthly life. You will be right in saying that such contact is continuous. Not a single earthly action remains unanswered on the part of the Subtle World. Each earthly thought arouses either joy and assistance, or malevolence and destructive sendings from the Subtle World. Even the weak spirits vigilantly attend earthly thoughts. Of course, powerful earthly thoughts inject a deepened vibration into the Subtle World, therefore it is but natural that the Subtle World should resound also to the earthly thoughts. When I say that the fall of a feather from the wing of a little bird causes thunder in the distant worlds, this is not a symbol, but only a reminder of the cooperation of all that exists. One needs to accustom oneself to the fact that there is no void. One must greatly strengthen one's conviction of the importance of man's task, his obligation and duty.

When man takes upon himself communion with the Higher World, he is truly daring, but this daring is sacred. The Subtle World listens to these calls and understands their significance. Such communion attracts a multitude of listeners—co-workers, as it were—therefore egoism must be excluded from prayer; for the best prayer will be renunciation and desire for the Good.

Let the Teaching persist in emphasizing the usefulness of the bond with the Higher World; only thus is it possible to affirm Great Service.

106. Let us not grieve if a response does not always come. Let us not be surprised if a response reaches us in an unexpected hour. Let us learn to understand supermundane conditions, and mainly let us comprehend the great invisible labor. But you already understand the Forces of the Higher World know no rest. Let such luminous Power guide each wayfarer in the night hour.

107. Light-mindedness, curiosity, suspicion, and unbelief are all of the same dark family. Imagine a great mathematician developing complicated formulae before children of elementary age. They will not only fail to grasp the great problems, but they will immediately fall into a derisive snickering. Thus, when someone approaches the Higher World out of curiosity, one can expect all consequences in the way of doubt and treason. If the consciousness is at a level that permits curiosity where there should be reverence for the greatness, there cosmic dross must be anticipated. Is it possible to approach the Higher World out of curiosity? Rather put the hand into the fire; thus let suspicion be charred!

In the heart one must bear reverence for the Higher World as the most important and beautiful fact in earthly life.

108. Someone may say that already he has often heard such calls to the higher worlds. So much the worse for him to remain deaf afterwards, for such deafness is impermissible. Nevertheless many regard such calls as out of place in business life; thus, people are far from the true understanding of Be-ness, notwithstanding the millions of years of the planet's existence. The more resonantly let us send forth our call to the Higher World.

109. Licentiousness and coarseness have now reached incredible limits. Savagery has finally broken into the cities and disrupted all the implantations of the spirit. The consciousness of the majority has returned to the darkest age. The clatter of the machine drowns the wail of the spirit. Therefore, each call to the Higher World is a call for salvation.

110. Complete attainment is possible only through complete trust. Only the realization of such completeness can bring one closer to achievement. It is impossible to impart from without what full trust is; only the heart can help one find this salutary path.

The Guru is in no need of reverence, but trust in the Teacher will be the sole vital bond with the Higher World. Realizing the value of trust here on Earth, one may apply the same measure of trust through all Hierarchy. It is right that reverence for the Guru be the firm foundation of an entire people. Destruction of respect for the Guru will also be the cessation of achievements.

Thus let us remember about full trust.

111. The Higher World has been in the foundation of all human, state, and social structures. Even if people are unaware of the primary origin of their social organizations, yet in transitory conditions may be seen traces of the living connection with the Higher World. One should not diminish the antiquity of the planet and of life upon it; it would be more correct to increase this figure. But let us not forget that continents have shifted their positions many times, and even at present one can still see near the poles a great many opportunities for discovery. Therefore, let us be cautious in limiting the earthly problem. Antecedent to savages we shall see traces of wise peoples who have vanished. According to surviving records of laws it is possible to affirm that the impulse toward comprehension of the Higher World has been manifested from time immemorial.

112. It is rightly understood that so-called sacred animals were not deities, but were a natural consequence arising from local conditions. Even now people often speak about some sacred obligation meaning thereby, not a religious rite, but a useful moral action. The conditions of antiquity often required a special attention to certain animals, or trees and plants. Sacredness signified inviolability. Thus was preserved something rare and necessary. The very same protection contemporary people call "preserves." Thus, one should refer very carefully to concepts that are not clear. So much has been added to the province of religion that, because of its antiquity, superficial observers are completely unable to distinguish the fundamental from the stratifications around it. The temple even now is a gathering place where, along with ceremony, barter and sale take place, and local matters are discussed. The same piling up of confusion is still taking place. Therefore let us not be excessively harsh toward the term sacred animals and other long-forgotten archaic symbols.

113. Prayer must be joyful, for communion with the Higher World will actually be full of ecstasy and solemnity. But such joy will be a special wisdom. It is possible only through realization of goal-fitness. It will be salutary through fullness of trust. It resounds with courage when the path is one.

Much is said about Samadhi, but have many experienced the different degrees of such ecstasy? Such joy liberates from all sorrow, therefore this path of joy is the path of Truth.

114. Aum has been explained in detail in various writings. The subtlety of vibrations, the wisdom of the sounding, and the beauty of the structure have long been known, but if the heart be dead, even such a "sesame" will not open the lock.

Again it is necessary to remind one about co-measurement and the fortifying of the essence of the heart. Aum is not accessible to heartlessness.

115. One of the reasons why Samadhi occurs so rarely is because people do not know how to deal with such an exalted state. They endeavor to interrupt the beginning of each unusual condition. Furthermore, people will not leave in peace one who is falling into Samadhi, and by their crudeness induce a dangerous shock. Yet in the most ordinary life a careful attitude of one to another is required. A man who has received a shock should be left in quiet. But rarely do people observe even such an elementary caution.

Thus it is impossible to safely bestow Samadhi so long as human thinking fails to understand how to deal with the higher energies. Therefore, every thought about the reality of the Higher World is in itself beneficial.

116. Great Service has all humanity in view. Neither nationality nor any other divisions should place limits on Service for the Good. It is not easy to avoid the various stratifications created through millennia. Only the realization of the Higher World can help to conquer all the survivals of superstition and atavism. Moreover one should not be arbitrary in feelings regarding karmic prejudices. Justice, even under unfavorable conditions, nevertheless indicates a just discernment. The individual as a responsible unit will be the object of judgment. It is difficult to evaluate an individual over and above all conventionalities, but devotion to Service will open one's eyes and enable one to perceive very clearly the seed of the spirit.

Thus the Higher World, and it alone, will bestow the higher judgment.

117. Tears and saliva alter their composition according to the state of the spirit. And each breath is different in its chemism. If ordinary breathing is not easy to investigate because of its superficiality, then a sigh which causes a tremor of the organism will be indicative. It can be noticed that a deep sigh sometimes causes something in the nature of an internal spasm. Such nerve contractions indicate increased outpouring of psychic energy. Depending on the impulse, it will stimulate the action of certain organs which will give a particular chemism to the breath. At the pronunciation of Aum a breath is manifested, the chemism of which will be very beneficial.

118. There are some who suppose that man is continuously dying; others know that man is incessantly reborn. The former are motivated by fear, the latter by joy. The former suggest death to themselves, the latter recognize life. Thus, man to a large extent predetermines his own future. One may be confident that he who destines death for himself does not know about the Higher World. He may display outward ritual, but his heart is far from the truth.

Affirmation of life is affirmation of Light. The human spirit is immortal, but such a simple truth is not close to people; for they care more about the body than about the spirit.

119. Life obliges man to ascend, whereas death is a descent. People, in principle, prefer to understand death as destruction. Existence itself affirms eternal renewal. Each man dies for yesterday and is regenerated for tomorrow. Each day a renewal of all three principles takes place. Each day and hour man draws nearer to or recedes from the Higher World.

Let each one by the quality of his thinking further his own ascent and his perception of the Higher World.

120. Tranquillity is the crown of the spirit.

121. Many qualities are inherent in the aura. They

are measured not only according to the size of the aura, but also by its inner tension. Indeed, the highly tensed aura is both the best shield and the most potent influence on its surroundings or environment. Sometimes radiations are good in color, but are not sufficiently intense.

Strengthening of the aura occurs through communion with the Higher World, as egoism falls away and selflessness is kindled. Thus, each communion with the Higher World will induce a strengthening of radiations. This subject invites scientific observation.

122. During communion with the Higher World it is actually possible to observe that bent or crossed legs have a deep significance. Let physicians examine what influence such a position of the extremities has upon the blood circulation and the nerve centers. Let them pay attention also to the respiratory channels. Whoever has understood the lubrication of the passages of the respiratory organs has already discerned the significance of these conduits.

123. Indispensable is the participation of the wise physician in all especially beneficial manifestations. Let it not be thought that We evade scientific observations; on the contrary, We value each scientifically founded thought.

124. In the face of danger human forces are multiplied in tension, likewise the state of ecstasy produces an influx of superearthly forces. If such a tension has been established, it is then possible to prolong this moment, in other words, man may receive a continuous increase of forces. It is only necessary that the Source of Forces become constant and near for him. Thus, the question of realization of the Higher World becomes urgent, and science itself will approach it as the impelling force of evolution. One may not only dream about such a bond of closeness but it is also possible to approach the Higher World by earthly measures. Each rapprochement of the worlds is already a victory over the flesh.

125. World events often occur, not because of actions themselves, but under the signs of the approach of the actions. People create a great deal under the sign of joy when as yet there is no apparent cause; and under the sign of terror or war when war has not yet broken out. Much is accomplished merely under the signs, therefore such reflexes acquire a most important significance for the alteration of life. Many examples of this can be cited. What is the need of war itself with all its disasters, if a single mirage can intensify energy? Much is actually constructed under the impetus of a mirage. Maya can sometimes be a most powerful impellent.

Therefore it is necessary to examine so attentively the guiding signs. The manifestation of improvement in understanding such signs actually hastens evolution.

Hence, let the most important be the guiding Principle.

126. If one succeeds in producing some action under a mere sign, it is very fortunate. The greatest reconstructions take place imperceptibly; only the result shows how much has been achieved. Thus, in everything actions under signs can be seen. The concept of the symbol is nothing but a reminder about a sign. The success of entire nations takes place under a symbol.

I consider it possible to proceed under the Higher Sign during the most perilous crossings.

127. Realization of the Higher World should arise freely, voluntarily and benevolently. Coercion is unfitting in such a transcendent matter. Thus, each teacher should interpret the Higher World as a higher joy. No one will call joy coercion. No one will condemn him who brings true joy. Yet how much inspiration must one develop in oneself in order to be a harbinger of joy! If a teacher has attained such a degree, he merits all reverence.

The Higher World is the touchstone of consciousness.

128. Why is treachery toward one's Guru such a revolting crime? During the first three years one may affirm one's consciousness, but after that the selection of the Guru becomes final. Such a law has deep significance. The Guru is the bridge to cognition of the Higher World. Such an earthly step easily establishes a relationship with the Higher World, therefore it is inadmissible to choose the Guru and then betray him; this would mean severing the bond with the Higher World forever. One can fall under the darkest influence when the saving thread has been broken. Such people are still able to move, eat, sleep, and slander, but the leprous infection may already have taken root. Likewise, traitors can still vegetate, but human dignity has been lost. Thus one can observe the wise laws which lay the foundation for living steps to the Higher World.

129. One must rejoice at the approach of each physician who desires to study the foundations of the rapprochement of the worlds. When the triple sign leads to triunity, then observations upon the human organism become necessary and undeferrable. The basis of threefoldness can be expressed throughout the organism. The physician must be informed about the Subtle World and the Higher World. Only from such considerations can he apprehend the subtlest conditions of the organism. And for him Aum will not be an empty sound.

130. If one would take note of even the external events of this year, he would get a most remarkable record of the course of world conflicts. Indeed, though this be only a collection of external signs, such a table would be a historic document of the highest significance. Of course, the external signs will be but sparks of the inner movements, and only the most devoted ones will not be frightened by such terrifying perturbations.

It is also possible to observe the connection of certain persons with world events. No one can understand how a world movement is personified in some individuals.

131. An alarmed child nestles close to its mother's knee, not in supplication but with a feeling of firm support and protection. Likewise, sooner or later, a man in distress turns to the Higher World. He will have nowhere else to go; he may be confused by the advice of uninvited bystanders, but his heart will be secretly atremble about the Highest.

132. Besides many definitions of the word Aum let us recollect that: A is Thought—the Basis; U is Light—the Primary Cause; M is Mystery—the Sacred.

133. Again one is asked, "Why continue to speak of three aspects when there are known to be more?" One should firmly point out that two paths exist—the path of analysis and the path of synthesis. Many intermediate conditions may be found so that the worlds appear as one connected whole. But later it is again necessary to separate the principal groups, and then we shall return to the triple structure.

Even upon Earth an enormous variety of degrees of spirituality can be perceived. One can see how people sometimes almost contact the Subtle World, since the consciousness in certain strata of the Subtle World does not transcend the earthly consciousness. Thus, the worlds are not only in contact but even overlap one another. The law of consecutiveness is firmly expressed in all nature. Even cataclysms, which seemingly are beyond the bounds of the spheres, primarily respond to some rhythm outside Earth.

Thus, let us not isolate where a just grouping is right. Man has departed so far from clear concepts that he must enter through the simplest Gates.

134. A real cognition and realization of the Higher World is indispensable to man. Religions have caused the most terrible wars. The most shocking cruelty has arisen from spasmodic thoughts about the Higher World. Such a horrible condition indicates that the Higher World is not understood in all its magnitude.

Realization of the great World of Beauty will result in a current of true thinking. Not a slayer but a wise creator is he who cognizes the Higher World. In the spirit, upon the summit, man can partake of communion with the Higher Power.

Thus, only a real comprehension of the Higher World will bestow equilibrium upon humanity.

135. Equilibrium constitutes the foundation of Existence. When, then, does man lose equilibrium in earthly life? When he is distraught and ill, then he staggers and proceeds gropingly, clutching at any and all objects. Does not the same thing occur when man is spiritually ill and loses equilibrium in his relationship with the Higher World?

Question people of different beliefs as to the firmness of their conception of the Higher World. You will receive a multitude of the most evasive replies. Many will refuse to answer at all, screening themselves by a hypocritical reluctance to talk about such a subject. Others will repeat memorized formulae which do not live in their hearts. A third group will affirm that the world was created two thousand years B.C. Thus, instead of spiritualized responses full of love and solemnity, you may receive heaps of dry leaves.

Meanwhile, life itself, as a reflection of invisible existence, should stimulate the consciousness of man. Half of life is given over to a mysterious condition which has not been explained by science. Moreover, each sensitive ear and eye can notice much beyond the province of everyday life.

People call indifference and stolidity "equilibrium," but nature itself whispers that equilibrium is tension. Consider tension to be the approach to the path of discoveries.

136. In the midst of the loftiest words remember that in each donation a part of that which is received should be allotted for the common use. Not only materially but also spiritually must this basic principle be understood as the law leading to equilibrium.

137. The inhabitance of heavenly bodies remains under doubt to this day. Even the best astronomers hesitate to express an opinion about this question. The reason lies chiefly in the conceit of man. He does not wish to admit incarnation in any conditions other than earthly. Fear before Infinity is also a hindrance. Surely, not many dare to reflect about such a remote giant as Antares, which, in the ocean of the Milky Way, presupposes beyond itself infinite Space. Meanwhile, people should think of distant worlds as being inhabited.

People cannot approach them in the earthly state, yet in the subtle body the best spirits have already approached such planets and brought back remembrances about their surface structure, coloration and inhabitants. Such experiences are rare, still they occur. They can reinforce the consciousness about infinite reality. In addition to the three invisible worlds it is necessary to recognize inhabited worlds. It is necessary to understand these oceans of thought which generate the music of the spheres. Thus let us diligently direct our thought to the distant friends and co-workers and Protectors. The thought that distant worlds are populated is not a supernatural fantasy. Man will firmly tread the earthly path when knowing about the surrounding magnitude.

138. More than once have the wise ones advised keeping closer to Earth. Will not such counsel contradict thoughts about Infinity? Not at all. We have been incarnated on Earth, and for this the causes are many. If our vigil is to guard Earth we must also love it. It is impossible to care for that which is not loved.

Earth itself is still full of unexhausted riches. It is possible to strengthen the planet by perfecting its health. Amidst healthy conditions on Earth one should not forget the Higher Magnitude. Thus will true equilibrium come about.

139. In the world treasury there are many teachings and legends which affirm the Higher World. People cannot justify themselves by pleading a lack of indications guiding them to knowledge. It is usual to hear complaints of the lack of knowledge as to the path to the Higher World. Such laments are hypocritical! These disgruntled ones will not take the trouble to seek out the Source. One may notice to what an extent aspiring people, even under the most unfavorable conditions, find strength to discover the Light. We watch over such light-bearers who overcome the most incredible difficulties.

The Law has been sent; the Path has been indicated; let him who seeks find.

140. Thought is the true friend of the seeker. Thought rules everything. Thought is inherent in each movement of the muscles. Thought leads and affirms. Thought finds the paths to the Teachings and the Decrees. Thought, if not scorned, teaches discrimination between the higher and the lower. Thought lives on perpetually and infinitely. It affirms movement and the realization of rhythm. Thought does not forsake one by day, nor by night. Thought uplifts the consciousness when the process of thinking becomes cherished.

141. Each instant man either creates or destroys. The world is filled with conflicting thoughts. A multitude of illnesses have been implanted by thoughts of destruction. A great number of murders take place at long distances from thoughts or from intersecting thoughts, but it is almost impossible to make man realize that his pre-eminence lies in continuous thinking. It is impossible to impress upon man how responsible he is for the quality of his thinking. The heart beats unceasingly, equally incessant is the pulse of thought. But it is not customary to talk about this.

Man either creates or destroys.

142. Madmen, they know not what they possess! People usually censure profligacy, yet is not thought being dissipated? Is not the great gift, attained with such difficulty, being reduced to nought? Thought, as the great gift of the Teacher, perishes in ignorant actions. Thus, men are ready to betray even their own planet, provided they do not have to think.

We already have pointed out the significance of thoughts many times, and again We shall return to the same subject. It is necessary to repeat a dose of medicine to an ailing man, so We weary not of affirming the first fundamental—Aum!

143. Now let us turn to the second sign of the Triune name, to the Primary Cause—Light. People have so confused the concept of Light with lighting that they cannot imagine Light as energy. Let us not look into that Infinity where thought and Light and all that exists merge into unity, but according to the earthly understanding let us apprehend Light as a salutary energy, without which life is impossible. Light is the most pervasive messenger of salvation. One can distinctly comprehend a difference between utilitarian fire and cosmic Light. Not fire, but radiance surrounds each living being. The benevolent thinker is surrounded by a rainbow, and through his light brings healing. So many times We have foretold the future of these radiations. We have said that with such a criterion the very structure of life will be transformed. One may rightly call Light the principle which leads to regeneration. Thought and Light are so closely linked that thought may be called luminiferous.

144. Utter darkness!—thus exclaims a man who falls into despair. The light has gone out—says the man who loses hope. Absolutely everything which refers to the luminous future is connected with Light. But people do not know how to rejoice at Light as energy. In the application of light treatments without using the opportunity to explain the significance of Light the physician and scholar are equally guilty. The ray of light acts on everything—muscles, bones and nerves. The brain lives by means of light; the vital substance of the brain is in need of rays of light. One can enumerate all the physiological conditions, and they will prove the Teaching of Light.

One should develop concentration in order to

observe what a remarkable exchange takes place between the radiations of thinking beings and the external rays of Infinity—the spatial rays are stretched like silvery threads. Condensation of light can be seen in electrical manifestations. The hand of man evokes a miraculous fire from space. You know that from a single touch flashes out a flame that does not burn. Such manifestations are rare, yet they do occur, and they indicate how much significance the bond of higher spirituality has during a transmission of spatial current. But it is necessary to take such signs with complete calm. Light does not coalesce with irritation and fear.

145. Fear and terror form a peculiar magnet. One may surmise what is attracted by such a dark magnet! People observe that fear darkens the sight. Indeed, darkness advances upon one possessed by terror.

Each instant man is evoking Light or darkness.

146. The light of the Subtle World has no relationship to the earthly understanding of solar light. In the lower strata, darkened consciousnesses create obscurity, but the higher the consciousness and thought, the more luminous is the miraculous radiance. Indeed, the dwellers of the Subtle World see both the earth and the luminaries, but the earthly lights are transmuted by their consciousness differently. Likewise with the thoughts of the Subtle World; though they are based on the same energy, their process is original. The law of equilibrium normalizes mental excesses.

147. In the purest place, the purest snow is saturated with earthly and cosmic dust; thus is space filled, even when crudely examined. Add a multitude of currents and rays, and you obtain an image of reality; thus are incarnate beings surrounded. Thoughts flow incessantly from the Subtle World; sometimes a man turns around and cries out at the impact of thought, but he still does not think of it as something coming from without. Man sees sparks and even fiery flashes, but he attributes them only to himself. It is impossible to teach men to treat their surroundings with respect. To such an extent do people fail to understand equilibrium that they either fall into sanctimoniousness or swell with conceit. For this reason the bridge to the distant worlds is difficult for people.

148. The third sign, the Sacred Mystery, is cognized by but a few. Light-mindedness whispers that everything pertaining to Mystery is unnecessary. Conceit suggests that all should be accessible, but man, blinded by lightning, cries out at the insupportable Light. Man, weighed down by the grandeur of thought, complains of the impossibility of containing it. Truly, the Mystery is commensurateness, which bestows the possibility of ascending without staggering.

By Mystery is the world maintained. There is no limit to Infinity.

149. Secrecy is also cautiousness and goal-fitness. One should plant flowers in appropriate soil. One should know when and to whom to intrust the seeds; thus does the concept of the Guru grow. In the simplest and most needed manner, the Guru tells what is especially necessary. If he guards the secret, it means that this is temporarily imperative. There can be no suspicion that the Guru conceals harmfully. One must accept the Guru as Guide; in such a manner the concept of the secret is transformed.

It is very important to assimilate the fact that the so-called Great Mystery is not an obstacle, but only the guarding of the path. If it is because of mistrust and fear that a man has not yet started his journey, then no measure will advance him. On such a path the wayfarer turns back, but to retreat is abhorrent. Therefore, the Guru helps find the best path. He will explain secrecy as an undefiled treasure.

150. Loss of co-measurement is loss of the path. Can that which is unknown be disproved? Can finiteness be affirmed in the face of Infinity? Can slander be admitted when the subject of the discourse is unknown? Can one oppose all Light and all thought? As madness darkens one's reason, so does treachery against the path of Light cast one into darkness.

151. The names of traitors are also recorded in the history of mankind. But where can traitors hide in the Subtle World, when their memory has been clarified? Not shame before others, but the unquenchable bitterness of infamy in the heart drives the traitors into ice and flame. And where are those who whispered treacheries into their ears? Why do they not succor their issue? They do not seek them out in the darkness. Terrible is the condition of traitors—murderers of body and spirit!

152. One should not spill poison carelessly. A great many may be infected, and no one will know where the poison may spread. Dark poisoners, do you know all your victims? But you will not remain ignorant. Sight will be given you, and you will see the entire scope of your doings. Thus do poisoners condemn themselves.

153. Each man bears a secret within himself. Rarely does the curtain of the past roll back—only when subtle energy abounds during one's earthly life. Only by transcending the boundary of Earth is man enlightened in the realization of a portion of his secret. Remarkable is the process when subtle energy reveals the Chalice of accumulations; the memory is suddenly illumined, and the past stands out in all justice. Amazing is the extent of man's transformation at the moment when he

leaves the earthly sphere. People call this death, but it is really birth; therefore, how pitiful it is when the subtle body sojourns long in sleep. Especially noteworthy is the transition wherein consciousness is preserved. Then it can be clearly imagined how the earthly tatters fall off and the imperishable accumulation emerges, revealing itself to be a true treasure. It can be understood why this most subtle treasure cannot be revealed amid crude conditions.

154. People can refine earthly conditions. The way lies not through riches nor power, but through the tremor of solemnity that is within reach of those chosen sensitive ones. Each such higher tremor is in itself a victory over the flesh.

On holidays the ancient weaving is taken out of the secret coffer. One cannot expose the finest work to a violent hurricane every day. One can rejoice when labor produces the higher joy in earthly life.

155. Besides earthquakes, there can be atmospheric disturbances. There can be concussions, as it were, during which the earthly sphere is agitated. These are caused not only by the crossing of currents, but also by conditions in the Subtle World. During discoveries, frequently something inexplicable is felt. This may be a reminder of the invisible world, full of energy. I would suggest that writers collect such unknown facts; thus will be accumulated a book of new juxtapositions.

156. If the Subtle World influences are so frequent, deep and lengthy relations should be established between co-workers of the two worlds. And so it is. Besides, the relationships are not so much a matter of blood kinship as of spiritual kinship. Often such co-workers meet also on the earthly plane; though they may be separated by differences of nationality and circumstance, yet an inner feeling will draw them together. Between them a confidence will be established very easily, though there may also be reverse exceptions. Ingratitude constitutes sinking into darkness.

157. The life of the planet may be understood as the sum total of all beginnings created with it. So much the greater is the responsibility of all thinking inhabitants of the planet. It is presumed that they are the crown of the planet, but if lumps of coal are found in the crown instead of precious stones, the resulting damage will be on a planetary scale. As a result, all the connecting currents will be destroyed.

158. When I speak about relations with the Subtle World, I do not advise artificial measures for such relations. These relations exist naturally throughout life. One should merely learn to observe them soberly; without any narcotics it is possible to observe around oneself many signs that clearly come from beyond the limits of narrow earthly existence.

It is necessary to understand to what an extent such natural observations can broaden the human concept of life. Prayer is transformed into spiritual communion, and reverence will not be dogmatic but vital and filled with love.

Without love there is no creation.

159. One may rejoice at that which finds a place in the heart, in other words, that which is loved. Is it possible without love to speak of signs about thought, about the Mystery, about Light? Mystery will turn into concealment, thought into scheming, and the Light into a firebrand; it is possible thus to distort the most Beautiful. But the true path achieved through love admits of no sacrilege. That which is visionary is turned into reality; the clamor of bargaining will find its proper place; man will realize the significance of solemnity.

Thus will Great Service begin to shine.

160. Sometimes you are absent, as it were, from current life. Sometimes you can hear the sounding of the distant worlds. Sometimes you can sense the air and the aroma of remote localities; you affirm immeasurable manifestations amid daily life. Indeed, you do not deceive yourself in sensing these fleeting contacts, which demonstrate how powerful the human being is. One cannot force oneself to sense such calls of Space, they reach only open hearts. Wiseacres attempt to show that such sensations are only autosuggestions, but for each autosuggestion a mental command must be sent in advance. However, you know perfectly well that such straight-knowledge arrives unexpectedly, beyond human imagination. You are transported into remote countries—manifestations of the spirit are swift as light. Thus it is possible to begin to realize the speed of movement in the Subtle World.

161. For each true discernment there is needed full confidence and spontaneity. One should strongly affirm these concepts as the basis of progress. It is possible to demonstrate how mistrust and artificiality will be the worst enemies. They swallow up vital energy. They are as sharp obstacles. How much force must be applied to continue the path with fatal leaps! Therefore, the sacred sounding can turn thought back to the fundamental and to the Light.

Thus let us conquer all obstacles and grow to love them. We shall not speak at length about that which one must love, because the heart knows.

162. Darkness is finite, but Light is manifested infinitely. Each one who knows this simplest of truths is already invincible. Any admission that Light is weak and the darkness great makes victory impossible. No matter what is given to the one of little faith, he drowns all in the ocean of darkness. Thus, let us take up the weapon of Light as the surest.

163. One should study the manifestations of nature in connection with world events. There may be found characteristic conformities; they repeatedly show how much of a living organism is the planet. Everything related to the planet is coordinated as the organs of a single body, therefore it is impossible to regard each being as an isolated individual. All beings belong to one organization, and they must regard themselves as responsible members of a community. In such a manner can one observe the fully defined structure of the Universe.

One need not be surprised at the continual attempts to rebel against the law of order. The force of chaos is like a maelstrom, and weak consciousnesses easily fall victims to such an epidemic. Indeed, one should look upon the influxes of chaos as infectious epidemics.

Observe and compare events. These observations help one to understand the laws of conformity and concatenation. The Teaching gives intimations which are confirmed by reality.

164. Why do physicians pay so little attention to atmospheric pressure? They send patients to health resorts or to the seashore or to the mountains, but they do not forewarn them that the quality of the air may be completely altered by reason of the effect of currents. There exist various bureaus and scientific observation posts, but they should also broadcast information useful to the medical profession. Good health must be protected by the state.

165. It has been correctly observed that great Influences come by special paths. Often people will be outwardly rebellious, and yet will accept what is sent. It is important to Us that that which has occurred be useful. One should not insist that that which takes place be judged according to present day standard—what is important is the result. We must be tolerant and pay no attention to lack of knowledge and to crudity. Therefore, one should pay attention to the essential nature of that which occurs.

166. I consider it possible to direct children from their earliest years to a realization of the Higher World. This is not compulsion, for it will help children to retain easily in mind much that otherwise might be quickly forgotten. Besides, such a manifestation will awaken incomparably beautiful forms. People strive for beauty and solemnity, on such basis it is possible to tell about the supernal Magnitude. One should not tear away countries from their best accumulations—each nation has its own expression.

The surmounting of limitations is possible only through the broadening of consciousness. One needs to know how to cautiously approach the heart of humanity through expansion of consciousness. Already many boundaries are being erased, but for such new paths a special love of mankind is required. It is necessary to cultivate this quality along with purity of body and spirit. Let hygiene of the spirit have a place in the schools, then lofty communions will become the best hours.

167. Life requires no temptations. Life can be transmuted under any and all conditions. Community of spirit is highest transmutation of life. Many of the ignorant do not wish to understand that community of spirit does not depend upon external form. It is created there where the concept of the broadening of consciousness is alive.

168. Community of spirit is possible where there exists a living magnet, then it is possible across all earthly boundaries to closely join each community. When a community lives in the sole service of Truth there exist no obstacles, and a special mutual help will be a natural expression.

Gratitude grows without compulsion, therefore the manifestation of joy especially affirms community of spirit—everyone would like to do something better.

169. One should reread books about principles and fundamentals. In general, it is necessary to renew one's impression of what has been read. It is wrong to think that a book read three years ago will not appear new on subsequent reading. A man himself changes in these years. His consciousness and understanding cannot remain on the same level; in all his surroundings change has taken place, and he would be unable to return to former conditions. Through his broadened horizon man discovers new contents in the book. Therefore, a book once read should not be cast into oblivion forever; knowledge lives on, and each sign of it must be alive.

170. Man does not know wherein lies his best action; therefore, to pride oneself on one's actions is ignorance. Human deeds depend upon many conditions. The distant worlds are either allies or adversaries. The causes and motives have been written down on such lengthy scrolls that the results cannot be read by human eyes.

Therefore, let us only apply all our forces and best strivings, leaving judgment to the Higher World.

171. Observe what takes place in your sensations during lofty communion. It can be noticed that feeling in the extremities is gradually lost, and finally the heart alone is sensed. This is not pain, but a sort of tension and imbuing. The communion can take place under any position of the body—standing, seated, or recumbent. The manifestation of the heart feeling referred to is called "the silver thread." It can wind and attract, as it were, and such a bond is a sign of nearness.

172. People often speak about doubles; it is as if they see their own selves. There are many explanations for such a manifestation. People usually forget the most natural one—actually the projection of the astral body. The subtle body is projected more often than is thought. It can acquire density, but is not usually seen by everyone; a degree of clairvoyance is required to see the subtle body. Furthermore, man can as easily see himself during a state of drowsiness as in wakefulness. Few pay any attention to the transitional state of drowsiness; yet precisely during this condition noteworthy manifestations occur.

However, man is not concerned in his ordinary life with such observations; either he completely denies the instructiveness of his sensations, or he yields to an artificial tension which cannot be considered natural. Hence, it is so necessary to seek equilibrium; if it is difficult to maintain it, then one should at least remember to strive for it.

173. People wish to render everything commonplace and insignificant, but when they see something that does not fit into their framework, confusion results instead of attention. The manifestation of such an unusual scale of events will actually be considered as mere chance. Thus are precious weavings senselessly torn asunder. The obviousness of events is often striking, yet words are found to violate even evidence. People know how to break up stone blocks and remain with a rubbish heap.

174. Humanity is wiping out the distinction

between tribes, therefore one should speak with special caution about tribes. Even those tribes that are still distinct in appearance and language are not basically and essentially isolated from each other. In conventional terms the subdivision is clear, but not in the matter of blood. An admixture is taking place which is so characteristic during a change of race. It is more appropriate to speak about humanity as a whole than to speak conventionally about the interlacing of branches.

It is significant to observe the oneness of the transmitted foundations. One should not forget the individualistic expression of each man, rarely will it be a tribal one. The history of each state shows how many wayfarers have crossed its land. Honest study leads one to contemplate mankind as a whole.

175. It is necessary to return often to the thought about humanity as a single heart. There is too much ignorance and impediment where there should be amiable cooperation. A history should be written of the subdivision of the heart of humanity.

176. In psychic investigation one absolutely essential thing has been forgotten—a comparison between the consciousness of the lowest savage and that of the loftiest thinker has never been introduced. Indeed, such a task requires lengthy observations. And the distinction between such consciousnesses will be striking. It will enable one to judge not only the multiple diversities of humanity but it will also direct thought to the consciousness of the animal and vegetable worlds.

In truth, animals have a developed consciousness. It is expressed not only in the domesticated state but precisely in the free life of wild beasts. Neither is it absurd to speak about the consciousness of plants. We already know about the nerves of plants, but more than that, it is possible to distinguish not only responsiveness to light but also attraction to a certain person. On the one hand there is human psychic energy, while on the other there is an affection toward a definite individual. It can be observed how plants, in order to please a beloved man, even bloom out of season. Many details can be drawn from direct observation.

It is Our wish to remind people that consciousness exists at a far greater depth than people suppose.

177. Minerals also have the embryo of consciousness, but the expression of it is too far removed from humanity.

It is possible to carry out many experiments in speech and thought, but such investigation requires prolonged time and special patience. Who will sacrifice himself for the purpose of tenaciously continuing observations without visible results? One should also know that results may appear in an unexpected place. Moreover, the laws of psychic energy are sometimes difficult to grasp. Their operation extends far beyond the scope of the human imagination.

178. Malice can be likened to rust.

179. It is impossible to dwell in malice without poisoning the consciousness. Not only bodily poison but a far worse decomposition is introduced by malice; the majority of cosmic dross originates from it. We cannot view with indifference a malicious destruction.

180. I have already spoken about the complexity of the laws of psychic energy. Recently there was an opportunity for you to be convinced of this once again. An individual, never having met a certain person, received psychic information about a memorable day connected with the latter. If one reflects about the goal-fitness of such attraction of man, one can understand the timeliness of such an action. Far away, a man receives psychic tidings, and by this very act a bond is established between distant parts of the world.

Therefore, psychic manifestations should be investigated over a broad expanse. It is difficult to corroborate the effects of psychic energy when there is no mutual exchange of information. Thus, physicians and scholars should meticulously compare facts.

181. Indeed, a noted physician treats cases not with medicines alone, but by psychic energy. Such manifested energy needs supplementing; this reinforcement proceeds out of the Ashram. Thus you see cooperation at long distances. Those who transmit the energy can only sense its outflow, but in their turn they receive a useful ray.

182. So-called symbolic dreams express in a lofty degree the bond with the invisible world. A consciousness cannot synthesize alone, it must receive an impulse from Above in order to see the future in a simple and clear symbol.

183. Again about reactions, or influences. You may have heard of an experiment of a certain chemist which illustrated the conflict of influences. He invited some friends to listen to some well-known authors; at the same time he prepared several chemical compounds conducive to laughter or tears, irritation or sympathy. In the midst of the most emotional passages of the reading the chemist filled the room with a contrasting gas. The result was that the listeners laughed during a funeral scene, wept during a joyful one and during a description of peaceful events they became bellicose. Thus, at the conclusion of the experiment it was strikingly apparent to what an extent words had been conquered by something unseen and unheard.

If even the comparatively crude reactions of gases can distort the reception of speech and the forms created by it, then how much stronger is the influence of the psychic energy of thought which itself creates forms!

Thus throughout life flow influences both coarse and sublime. It is right to know both the darkest obsession and the highest inspiration. Call them what you will, such influences do exist.

184. The experienced physician, extending medical aid, says to the patient, "Forget about your illness!" He knows that people do not usually know how to suggest to themselves recovery. Therefore it is better not to let them tire themselves with doubt as to their health. People could help their recovery by directing their forces toward healing, but they prefer to weaken themselves by not allowing nature to exercise its good action.

Is it not useful to remember about influences when we speak of the higher worlds?

185. He who transmits his influences does not always know what is being created. He notices that his energy has flowed out; he may sense a sudden weariness, but, like a generous donor, he does not know the measure of his benefactions. First, compassion is engendered, and then love for humanity.

He who loves has access to a higher communion.

186. When a man realizes all surrounding influences, he is then able to begin self-activity. He learns to discern where is the higher Hiero-inspiration and where low destruction. It is not so easy to distinguish all the cunning wiles, but it is fortunate when the heart is atremor with realization of usefulness to the Higher World.

Contacts with the Higher World are spread throughout life; even in small everyday matters the sparks of higher tension can be discerned. There are no actions which are not intensified if they touch the Higher World.

One should love such tension, for without it there can be no Great Service!

187. A man striving toward the Higher World will commit no bad deeds. The name alone—the Higher World, already indicates that everything connected with it is lofty. People may call such striving by different names, but its essence is one, and its activity is always useful to humanity. I do not speak of outer activity, but of the heart's fire which adorns each task with a radiant quality.

188. The smith strikes many sparks with his hammer. Let us not think of him as merely an unskilled workman. The time has come to revise castes. Their original meaning has become lost in the ages, and their effects are before everyone's eyes.

Therefore, let each heart offer its best thought to the Higher World.

189. The triple consonance is pronounced as "Om!" It is as if two letters merge together, but in reality the Basis and the First Cause are blended in the one Indivisible. One can observe everywhere how goal-fittingly the laws of consonance have been established.

190. For him who wishes an easy life it is better not to live. Let him not think about the Higher World who willfully demands rewards for his merits. Whoever reckons wealth in the material world is a pauper in the Higher World.

191. Let us not understand value by earthly measures only; those measures do not even apply in the Subtle World. Let us inure ourselves to broaden measures easily, otherwise even the smallest particles of space will crush us.

192. Let no one think that Our summons to the

Higher World means tearing one away from Earth. On the contrary, the greatness of the Higher World only affirms all other manifestations of life. Earth cannot be a negligible planet when it is enwrapped in the very energy which is filled with the higher Light. Each comparison with the Higher World also enhances the good quality of earthly thoughts. Only evil can separate the worlds; only ignorance can dismember manifestations; only non-understanding counsels that earthly life is no part of beautiful creativeness; therefore, let us direct all science toward a righteous cognition. Nothing can divert one's heart if devotion and the sense of beauty live in it.

193. The housewife who has churned from milk a morsel of butter has already become initiated into a very important aspect of cosmogony. Thus she can understand the generation of the heavenly bodies. Before beginning her churning the housewife thought about it, and only from a combination of thought and churning was the useful matter produced.

Subsequently cheese may be produced, already with the embryos of a population. Let us not smile at such a microcosm, the same energy evolves also the systems of worlds. It is necessary only steadfastly to realize the significance of thought, the significance of great energy. Is it not marvelous that this same energy glows in the heart of each man?

194. Experimenting upon letters has a great significance. If it is possible to show graphically that a manuscript has been saturated with psychic energy, then such a demonstration must necessarily be made use of upon other applications of the very same energy. Man saturates each object with his energy through contact. Furthermore, man leaves in everything his own characteristics. From letters it is possible to know the quality of the writer. This experiment can be developed by using other objects. The face of man is no secret.

195. While only one person is talking, many difficulties do not arise; but a congregation of any size is already full of difficulties. Indeed, by a single thought a man can violate the unity of any gathering. There have been attempts to unify the consciousnesses of people by various incenses and by the burning of resinous substances, but even such measures could not bring the gatherings into an exalted frame of mind. Thus, it is impossible by any sort of compulsion to attain the construction of the Temple of the Heart. Different ages and beliefs have not induced people to rally together for one exalted transport.

But one can picture a group of people assembling without compulsion; they can gradually conceive thought that leads to the Higher World. One may rejoice when people gather together in the name of the Good and resolve to bear this salutary Good on all paths.

I affirm that it is possible to accomplish a great number of useful actions when energy is not dissipated upon idle disputes and quarrels. How can there be higher communion, if brain and heart turn into a crimson flame? Even the very Battle for the Higher World will not generate crimson flame. The light of courage may glow ruby red, but every irritation will already be a weakening.

196. Kurukshetra is here on Earth. Armageddon is represented as an earthly field. The ancient holy wars of Babylon also have earthly designations. The most spiritual on Earth has been named.

Thus, let us realize the indivisibility of the worlds. When people will construct life upon the grandeur of indivisibility, they will transform the whole of Existence.

197. Sacrifice and assistance are created in secret, such is the nature of these actions. Only the Higher World knows who really helps whom. The sacrifices have been inscribed upon imperishable scrolls. Beautiful is the law of the secret heart sacrifice.

198. All faiths have forbidden pronouncing the Highest Name in vain, and this law is beautiful; in it is expressed the highest co-measurement. If even earthly children are protected then how careful one should be with the highest concept.

When I advised that co-measurement be inscribed on the pillar, anyone could understand the striking progression. And yet bipeds are found who place themselves upon the pedestal. Dark is the abyss of ignorance!

199. It has been said, "Many mothers, fathers, wives, sisters and brothers, will be given," yet even such a clear indication does not compel people to reflect as to where this will take place. They do not wish to meditate about earthly lives! The wisest principles do not reach ears that are closed.

200. Can evil ones possibly speak about Good?

Be disciples of knowledge and grow to love the Higher World.

201. Sparks of the laws of the Higher World have been generously strewn over the bosom of Earth. It is possible to gather them as the most precious treasures. Amid such harvests, all becomes beautiful. The highest goal-fitness adorns the coordinations of a free will that understands the complete coherence of the working parts. Verily, all life becomes a fulfillment of useful tasks entrusted by higher thought.

Not groveling toil, but heroic conquest will be the mark of Love, the victorious!

202. The kindling of the nerve centers has not sufficiently attracted the attention of physicians. It is very important to observe that the flaming of each center gives rise to symptoms of the local organ, yet the organ itself is not ill but is only vibrating in response to the fire of the center. It is possible to show that many false illnesses are announced by physicians when they do not recognize the basic cause of sensations. Moreover, the cause itself of inflammation is superficially studied. Purely cosmic conditions may be indicated, and of no less significance is the condition of the mass of humanity.

Those who take upon themselves the burden of Earth are like the symbol of the giant, Atlas. Such pillars of the world are very few in number; people should cherish them as lightning rods, but instead, at best, people chuckle over what seems to them hysteria and do not wish to know more about the basis of the manifestation.

Understanding cannot come so long as the three worlds and their inter-relationship are unrealized.

203. Is it possible to endure the siege of Earth, if Hierarchy is unrecognized? The Teaching of the Higher World is sent as a thread of salvation. Such a thread can be changed into a steadfast cable, yet earthly fires can burn through the strongest cable. Therefore, earthly fires can be of service to the Fire of the Higher World.

204. Whoever can hear the music of the spheres can also hear the wailings of space. Do not regard such wailings as abstract symbols, they are borne from both the Subtle World and Earth. Humanity may be asleep, but its heart can wail and moan. Many hearts are asleep in daily life, but when the mind does not interfere and consciousness awakens, the heart stands before reality. Not without reason was it said that people sleep by day but are vigilant by night.

According to the intensity of the wailings one can estimate the awakening of the consciousness of humanity. It wails when reality is revealed. It has also been said that the bazaar is the veil of reality. Under the dust of the manifested bazaar the heart becomes silent. It is necessary to be deeply conscious of the Higher World in order, by its signs, to know how to step through the mire of the street.

One should not fall into despair at the frightful lamentations of space. They express the confusion of the world, but you know how deep this confusion is. Whoever knows this is not disconcerted. Whoever is in contact in consciousness with the Higher World is steadfast and invincible; he has given freedom to his spirit, indestructible and reaching out into Infinity.

It is necessary that one be prepared to listen not only to the majestic music of the spheres but also to the cry of animal terror. It is impermissible to know only one side of existence. Only cognition of the whole Universe will give the affirmation of victory. The unwise are afraid of every darkness, but for him who realizes, even darkness is a contrasting background for Light. He who knows about the world of Light is not afraid of darkness.

Thus, it is necessary to appreciate the wondrous music of the spheres, and to understand that on this step are also heard the lamentations of the world.

205. If we collect the facts, we can apprehend the impetuousness of events. One can see what unprecedented events each hour brings.

206. During experiments upon psychic energy,

one should pay attention to the different shades of the manifestations. Primarily, observation will reveal a general design, but the attentive observer will detect a great number of original details. For example, you have discerned an unusual cruciform movement above the brain of the one observed. In reality, such a movement is very deplorable. It signifies either an advanced stage of obsession, or madness. Likewise one can also observe that in an extremely brief interval the reaction may be sharply altered. Therefore, it is necessary to carry out repeated observations. Psychic energy, like the waves of the ocean in its multiplicity of currents, is influenced by many conditions from within and without. It is very important to observe such temperature curves of the spirit. It is likewise important to observe when this same reaction appears—for both the living and the dead. The reasons for such manifestations are many. It may be that life has already flown away; it may be that obsession has obscured the basic nature; it may be that anger has extinguished all the centers; it may be that sickness is in possession of the organism; but in any case such a manifestation merits attention.

One may observe the expansion of the circle of consciousness, and such an achievement is cause for rejoicing. Likewise, it is necessary to pay attention to any trembling, stoppages, tremors, and digression from the precise forms. They depend upon the psychic condition and upon various illnesses. Therefore, it is necessary to observe both the healthy and the sick. It is possible to continue the same task with manuscripts, with colored surfaces, and in general with objects which have been in human hands.

In such a way, the question of the human aura and of human accumulations upon objects can receive a new impetus. Indeed, the possession of a clear consciousness by the observer himself can be of much assistance. Irritation is a poor conductor.

207. Aum, in its higher vibration, leads the consciousness into the best condition for observations upon psychic energy. One may rejoice when by simple methods it is possible to take up a very important and graphic experiment.

208. Thought about Us, as a purification of consciousness, can be likened to looking far into the distance. Then a person's spirit acquires a special courage, which abides in him and carries him through perils. Without the Higher World it is difficult to set forth on the path.

209. One need not be disturbed if the word physiology is applied to the Higher World. Truly, any conscious man could select a far better word, but for the average understanding neither matter nor physiology are untrue determinants. Matter is spirit, physiology is the law of Existence. No one can say that the spirit does not contain all. Physiology is only the conventional definitive of many operative laws.

Indeed, through deep study far more applicable names will be found. Even for the loftiest concepts it is possible to find comparisons in physical usage. People do not tightly cover an ailing tooth nor an open wound. They understand the need of admitting air in order not to deprive the affected part of a useful substance; likewise, the spiritual perception must not be deprived of communion with the Higher World. Just as bodily hygiene is indispensable for earthly life, so also is prophylaxis of the spirit needed. Do not be surprised that We apply medical terminology to the spirit; through this the physician may feel that his sphere is close to the Higher World. Let each one find the One Path in his own way, even though it be the way of mechanical terms.

210. Thus, free knowledge should not be prohibited. Such forbiddance is an evidence of ignorance. In the growth of knowledge is distinguished the true path. The more varied the investigations, the more beautiful the results. There can be no dark paths for the enlightened eye; it discerns a particular conclusiveness through investigation of the most diverse quests of humanity. We are not deniers, for negation does not permit profound study. Many hieroglyphs have been scattered throughout the world, but only in good will is it possible to approach the sacred signs.

211. It is necessary for people to free themselves from any arrogance in relation to all that is unknown to them. Thus, one can observe continually that the ignorant ones express themselves offensively about everything inaccessible to them. It is indispensable that the foremost scholars make themselves worthy examples of broadmindedness. Evolution is completely excluded where people do not recognize the possibilities of infinite cognition. I repeat, the success of perfection begins with self-perfection.

Each one who wishes to enlist in the Great Service must free himself from arrogance.

212. It is necessary to endeavor to find the simplest causes of manifestations. People notice that clair-audience is better at dawn. The reason advanced for this is far from the truth. They suppose that after the night the organism is rested; they think that the currents just before dawn lend assistance, but they overlook the simplest and most natural solution. Actually, the most obvious cause lies in the fact that during sleep man has contacted the Subtle World, and therein has enhanced his subtle qualities.

Similar comparisons may be adduced from many domains; yet all of them indicate only that man thinks too little about the higher worlds, and thus deprives himself of the truest solutions.

213. Sleep is participation in the life of the subtle sphere. The condition of sleep is significant from the point of view of psychic energy. It is undoubtedly strengthened, but in a special quality; in other words, it acquires the distinctive quality of the Subtle World.

214. There are people who refuse to understand what arrogance is. Let us help them understand by saying, "Do not belittle, and rid yourselves of the disgusting worm of disparagement." He who belittles is almost the equal of a traitor. In the presence of such vipers there can be no talk of communion with the Higher World. To reduce something to worthlessness is an unworthy transformation! He who dwells on the negligible will find himself on the path to nothingness. The higher communion is impossible with thoughts about the insignificant. It is possible to converse in the simplest expressions, but their meaning need not be insignificant. Whoever is preoccupied with representing his neighbor as a nonentity is measuring by his own insignificant standard.

215. One may meet people so hostile as to suspect something unfitting in the word Aum. They will ask, "Why have other beautiful symbols been forgotten? What is the purpose of not mentioning other exalted concepts?"

Let us say, "Nothing has been forgotten, nothing has been belittled, nothing has been destroyed. We are not disparagers, nor are We afflicted with arrogance. But no one can rob the concept, Aum, of its antiquity, with all its significant threefoldness. The primary signs should not be thrown aside. Instead of hostile ignorance, you had better manifest humaneness and show love for attainment of knowledge. Succeed through love!"

216. There are people who can detect radio waves without an apparatus. Taken alone, such a faculty represents no special achievement, but it furnishes a useful comparison with transmission of thought; the basic energy is identical. If the far cruder transmission of radio waves can be received, the next step is entirely possible. People are continually receiving thoughts from space and translating them into their own language; yet even such a simple truth needs to be repeated.

It is incomprehensible why people are so opposed to the simplest consideration—that of thought as energy. As if such a truth could demolish people's hearths! True, the energy can shake out some of the dust, but the house will be the purer for it.

Avoid no opportunity of speaking about thought as a motive force!

217. When the body has tired of one position, it is advisable to change to another. The same thing is true in all circumstances of life. Each change has its causes. Let us learn to deliberate about them, in this way each condition attests its advantages. Thus I repeat, affirming tolerance.

218. The foundation of life must be a clean one. True, certain bipeds pass their whole lives in mire; they somehow vegetate, but anyone who is accustomed to cleanliness stifles in filth.

It is exactly the same with food. For one who is accustomed to pure food, it is unhealthy to stuff oneself with impure decaying matter. Whoever has been accustomed from childhood to unclean food is not in immediate danger, but he must remember that the germs of the most terrible diseases are contained in impure foods. It is possible to postpone realization of this for a limited time only; eventually the sowing will yield its harvest.

219. Lethargy is a peculiar, undefined state between sleep and death. The heart almost stops, the body is motionless, and an unearthly expression of the face is maintained. Yet the man is not only alive but returns to wakefulness for a reason of his own, which no one understands. The falling of one into lethargy is unexpected, and the circumstances of such a transitory state can never be known to those around him. In Our language this is a protracted extrusion of the subtle body. Such a state is not a sickness, and should be looked upon as an unnatural tension of the organism in relation to the Subtle World. It may be the result of overfatigue, fright, shock by grief, or unexpected joy. Especially noteworthy is the instant of awakening. Usually those present create great harm by their untimely exclamations and questions. Each question of this kind is already a suggestion. One should take the greatest care not to dissipate the retained impressions. Most often, people emerging from lethargy begin to assure us that they remember nothing. Rather, such remembrances have been stricken from their consciousness by some inopportune questions or noise. In such a manner an opportunity of acquaintanceship with the Subtle World is lost. During the awakening, the aroma of attar of roses is very useful.

220. One should also pay attention to infantile eclampsia. It indicates development of the nerve centers. During such a state it is necessary to maintain special quietude. By nature such children are highly gifted, but the shield of the body must be strong. It is necessary to regard such manifestations as a seeming overfilling of the Chalice. Not without reason was this called in antiquity a "divine visitation." During such attacks, complete quiet of all surroundings, as well as warmth, the odor of rose oil, and a uniform temperature are essential. Certain peoples have made use of soothing music, and such an expedient was helpful; for the assistance given must be a psychic one.

221. Any nervous attack can be cured under conditions of quietude of surroundings and an even temperature, and through the influence of sound, color and aroma. But it is difficult to find such a combination of conditions. Moreover, it is absolutely necessary to apply that precise combination of sounds, color and aroma which is individually needed in such a state.

It is therefore very important that experiments on the effect of sound, color and aroma be carried out as extensively as possible. Even in schools many useful experiments could be conducted. It is difficult to find in private homes a special room with adequate accommodations for this, but schools and hospitals should have proper quarters with certain appliances. Thus it is possible to add to suggestion many contributory conditions.

222. It is possible to cure many cases of paralysis by means of intensified suggestion. The inception of many diseases, for example, cancer, tuberculosis, and stomach ulcers, can be arrested by suggestion strengthened by psychic influences. It can be observed that suffering caused by cancer is augmented by scarlet light, whereas violet has a soothing effect. Similarly with sounds, consonance in a major key will aid the action of the violet ray, but dissonance will increase the pain.

Let us not deprive physicians of opportunities for new discoveries. Let them investigate many combinations, but it is necessary to remind them of the most immediate path of science. When consonance will lie at the basis of the treatment, then one can imagine what subtlety of energy will be summoned to the assistance of humanity.

223. No one should call a psychic influence "sorcery." Such an ignorant opinion belongs to times long past. On the contrary, investigation of psychic energy is true progress.

224. The thought that psychic treatment has already been satisfactorily established is futile. Attempts to cure by means of light and sound have been weak and not synchronized. No one is occupied with the study of the correspondence of aroma to color and sound. But the principal error lies in the fact that there are almost no physicians who would understand the correspondence of the worlds. Without realization of these fundamentals it is possible to sink into the narrowly material plane, yet the sphere of psychic energy embraces all planes. It can be recognized only in all subtlety. Thus, the physician cannot speak about obsession if he himself has no conception of the Subtle World! The physician cannot understand treatment with light if he cannot distinguish the scale of colors. He who likes the crudest music cannot discriminate a refined tonality. He cannot prescribe treatment through aromas if he himself cannot distinguish them. My purpose is not to belittle physicians, on the contrary, I would wish to equip them for the saving of humanity. Poisons have increased too greatly. Many resources have been directed only to the destruction of psychic energy, so that not only in cities but also in the midst of nature prana is already being violated by the intrusion of extraneous currents. Meanwhile it is necessary for humanity to understand that it has no right to poison Earth's atmosphere; mankind is responsible for the hygiene of the planet.

It is desirable to ask physicians to give attentive understanding to the relationship of the worlds and to the refinement of their own senses. An evil person cannot speak about good. A coarse person cannot judge refinement.

225. After the recognition of hypnotic suggestion, one should begin to think of ways of strengthening it. But first it is necessary to realize all the stages of suggestion. If man is continually suggesting and under the influence of suggestion, then how attentively must one cultivate the ability to discriminate the degrees of earthly and subtle influences! For this, scientific research is needed in order that the scholar himself may cognize the gradations of the worlds. If he be a denier, then there will grow up a generation of ignoramuses.

226. In no medical school is psychology taught. Such a subject does not exist altogether. The word psychology is connected with pedagogy, but not with cognition of the qualities of psychic energy. It is unthinkable that medical instruction should neglect such a fundamental subject. The cognition of psychic energy permits due attention to be given to remedies. Much less medicine is required when physicians are able to apply psychic treatment. The introduction of assistance by psychic energy will renew all the manifestations of life. Let us not separate the higher concept of life from medical assistance. So many ancient sources point out that priests were also physicians. Thus it was emphasized that the physician must have authority, otherwise he would trail behind the diseases without the possibility of warding them off.

But a bold word needs to be found in order to

affirm the higher bond of the worlds as a guaranty of the health of people. There will be no health so long as people do not know why they bear the earthly burden. It is impossible to satisfy the consciousness within the sphere of one tiny planet. Terror will tear the heart that is deprived of the beautiful concept of unity of the worlds.

Let the physician, as a priest of science, be the one to bring the knowledge of the world of Light into the home.

227. Let people value every knowledge!

228. Let the ruler be the first to show respect for science, because often the ruler does not consider himself obligated to bow before knowledge.

Through knowledge, realization of the Higher World will enter anew. There is no other path!

229. Let people evince a desire not to vegetate but to become better. They forget the beautiful law of improvement. The word *evolution* is often understood as an imposed obligation, but the joy of improvement comes not from a thing imposed, it is indissoluble from the seed of the spirit. Only with this understanding is it possible to cross over all the chasms of darkness.

230. I always advise writing down various observations; from them, in time, a valuable chronicle may be compiled. Such writings are helpful in the study of the history of evolution. For example, I will remind you of one such writing. An experienced observer relates his meeting with a prominent leader: "During the conversation I observed that the latter seemed to be in a drowsy state. At the same time, around him could be distinguished an indistinct cloud which waved and moved about. One could understand that the subtle body had almost emerged from my companion; yet he was imperturbable, making plans for

his coming departure. Upon saying farewell, he drew a ring from his finger and suddenly asked me to take it in remembrance of him. Within three hours my friend was killed by an evil plotter. The question arises—if the subtle body witnessed the preparations for the murder, and the spirit already gave me the ring as a token, then why did not the consciousness also give warning of the plot? Evidently we have to do with a very complex law of the Higher Wisdom." Thus an observer wrote in the French language.

One may recall occasions when people were observed to express wonder as to why someone failed, as it were, to know the immediate future. One should understand the complexity of the laws of karma and of cognition in the subtle body.

231. It is very useful to study ancient languages; in them has been recorded the history of man's thoughts, and it is possible to follow the development and elimination of concepts. Let us take the Sanskrit and Latin languages. We can see to what extent the latter had already dispensed with profound concepts; but ancient Rome, aiming toward materialism, cannot be compared with the records of India's thought.

Language is the chronicle of a people; the dictionary is the history of culture.

232. The soul of a people is an open book. One should know how strongly it is reflected in each manifestation. Therefore, the study of a people is a science. Whoever wishes to peer into the future must know what gates can be opened. Goodness and confidence can be based upon knowledge of a people as a whole. It is possible to discern wherein lies the treasure and where the trash.

233. There is solace in the understanding of the

three worlds. Nothing else can appraise the wealth of Truth.

234. You undoubtedly will encounter this objection, "Why are the higher worlds and science spoken of on the same page?" Those who speak thus, fail to understand the Higher World and belittle science. People of such limited intelligence are very widely scattered, and because of their heartlessness are extremely malicious. They occupy various public posts and therefore are able to whisper in many places. To contradict them would be useless. Every man of heart will rejoice at each proper understanding of the Higher World. Each wise man esteems a word in the defense of science.

Of all earthly themes, love and creativeness are most closely combined with the concept of the Higher World. When mentioning the Higher World the worthy man will rejoice. In a discussion about science he will be heartily delighted. If both concepts provoke only condemnation, it will be the sign of a dead heart. Be not distressed at encountering deniers and condemners, this is just as unavoidable as is the fact of the existence of Light and darkness. Straight-knowledge will whisper where the degree of darkness makes further persuasion useless; sowing is advisable only on good soil. You already know that understanding friends arrive irrespective of earthly considerations. It happens that even the jinns build temples, but the Higher World and knowledge are inaccessible to them. Sooner or later they rebel and return into darkness. Shall one name examples!

Therefore, serve the Higher World and science. Through love in the light of knowledge let thought of the Higher World be clarified.

235. It is especially incomprehensible to see how

people often fall from reverence into disparagement. They try to represent the Inexpressible; a false countenance results, which only debases the lofty concept. Many such false representations have been scattered throughout the ages. People repeat about the invisible, and immediately proceed to imprison Light in petrified forms.

It is time to manifest commensurateness.

236. The Higher World is incorruptible, but instead of self-purification through thought and labor, people still try to bribe the Higher Grace. In such ignorance is expressed a complete unwillingness to reflect upon the essential nature of the worlds. The history of prayer shows that at first hymns were chanted, then prayers were spoken for all beings, and only later did man dare to importune with demands for himself. Sufficient evidences have been given as to how worthless for evolution is everything engendered by selfishness. One cannot purchase favor and justice. Is it not shameful that such words must be repeated?

One may ask oneself, Is not involution taking place? The end of Kali Yuga can also produce such manifestations. Terrible cataclysms have been indicated, but what can be more frightful than a catastrophe of the spirit. No earthquake can be compared with the dissolution of consciousness. All forces need to be intensified in order to hold back humanity from the abyss, therefore meditation about the Higher World is a necessity of the day.

237. It has been rightly observed that certain plants have the aroma of musk. It is useful to gather information about such plants. They will not possess all the valuable qualities of the life-giver, musk; nevertheless the useful quality of preserving vigor is inherent in them. One may sometimes observe that neighboring plants begin to take on the same scent; the roots and soil may serve as conductors.

238. The most complicated matter can be approached by the simplest path; the principle requisite is attentiveness. Even very experienced observers lose it amid common-placeness. But the Higher World requires love and gratitude. How otherwise is it possible to scan the subtle signs under incarnate conditions?

239. Everything in the world is unrepeatable. Hence it is possible to realize how much of the unusual there is. Without such understanding people will not discover their own earthly position. It is impossible to think about evolution if the impelling causes and the attainable goal are unknown. Earthly existence has no meaning without understanding of cause and effect. Yet if people would even partially realize the unusualness of their surroundings, they could more easily focus their thoughts upon the Higher World. It is impossible to persuade people to turn without a transitional step to so different a sphere as the Higher World. But if the eye gradually learns to distinguish the multiformity of its surroundings, it will more easily become accustomed to the discernment of subtle manifestations. Verily, everything must be cultivated.

240. It may be asked why people do not, in the material world, remember their subtle sojourns. One of the reasons why it is impossible to recall everything of the Subtle World is the impossibility of its being assimilated by our physical envelope. Indeed, the spirit could not undertake physical evolution if it could preserve within itself a recollection of the expanses of the Subtle World. Of course, it is sometimes possible to catch from the Subtle World a glimpse of the fiery grandeur which the world of flesh can realize only in the rarest cases. Only at times can even the best spirits recall their earthly existence, and extremely rarely do they remember their conditions in the Subtle World. Sometimes the projection of the subtle body brings back a certain realization of life in the Subtle World. But to remember subtle existences is very difficult and it is incompatible with earthly conditions.

241. It may be explained to you that the three letters Aum signify—past, present, and future. And such a meaning has a foundation. The Basis is the past, the Light is the present, and the approach to the Sacred is the future. Indeed, the sowers of various interpretations are mindful of the best explanations; but such explanations often are due to earthly understanding. Thought has no restriction as to the past, present, and future; it is as eternal as Infinity. To discuss Infinity, one must revise all measures; hence, the concepts of finite and infinite will expand. In the infinite there are no arbitrary interpretations, because in Infinity all is contained.

Therefore, when we speak of the magnitude of the fundamentals, let us beware of applying earthly measures. Let us especially not base our concepts on the finite, because, in essence, the finite does not exist.

242. Let thought attain useful flight. This striving needs to be cultivated lest distant expanses confuse the thinkers. Before he can feel himself a guest of all planets, man must accustom his consciousness to the small dimensions of Earth. Particular transgressions have been committed through an incommensurate concept of Earth and its place in the Universe. From this have arisen the obscuration of religions, ignorance in matters of government, and a prematurely ill-state. Therefore, thought must not only encompass Earth but must also love to soar to the distant worlds.

243. It would seem that what has been said is simple; why, then, is it so rarely applied? No abstraction is taught; no mere wandering of thoughts ordained. It is necessary to stimulate the striving of thought in all reality. But only a few comprehend the difference between abstractly wandering thought and real thought. Only in immutability can the Higher World shine.

Equally simple is the consideration of the saturated condition of space. Much has been written about this, nevertheless to the majority of people such information remains incomprehensible.

It is necessary to cultivate thought.

244. Much has been indicated about the necessity of developing patience; but wherein may there be discovered such a touchstone? It is useful to begin a conversation with the most bigoted denier. Let him expound his improbable devices; the patient thinker surmounts all ignorance without having recourse to denial. In the creativeness of his thinking, the thinker guards against irritation, during the lesson in patience one is not irritated. Let the ignorant lose their tempers, for they have no other answer, but the probationer in patience will not debase himself with the methods natural to the ignorant. Even in schools, tasks in patience should be proposed.

Without a realization of patience it is impossible to reflect on Infinity. The dimensions of the tasks of the Higher World require tests of patience.

245. Thinkers are subjected to many persecutions. But let the oppressed ones answer, "Though you persecute us, our thoughts are already sown, and nothing can erase thought in space." There is no point in exiling the thinker, his heritage is indestructible throughout all the worlds. Not only is thought indestructible but it even grows in space. The very departure of the thinker from the physical world only opens a broader domain for his thinking. Murderers and poisoners show little acumen; aiming to free themselves of the sowings of the thinker, by their very act they but strengthen him.

246. Many disciples gathered around a certain venerated teacher. They pursued their occupations successfully until a rumor reached them that in a distant city another teacher had made his appearance. This news gradually created doubt and divided opinion among the disciples; it weakened their attention and hindered their advancement.

One day the teacher said, "I am going into the mountains; in the meantime, strengthen yourselves in the assimilation of the Teaching." The teacher departed. But within a short time, unexpectedly, the disciples were visited by a new teacher with whom they were extremely delighted. Finally one disciple, hoping to flatter the new teacher, exclaimed, "How much more excellent and intelligible is your Teaching than the former one!" Then the new teacher removed his turban, threw open his garment, altered his facial expression, and the disciples recognized their former teacher. They became greatly abashed and whispered, "Why did you change your appearance?" He said to them, "You wished to have a new teacher and a superior Teaching, so I helped you in this." Thus one can discover in ancient tales qualities of people common to all ages.

247. One should not strive for the new merely by denying the basic. Cognition is Our advice and command. Cognition has nothing in common with treachery and blasphemy. Where foul speech makes its nest, do not look for true cognition. No one wishing to preserve a very delicate flower places it in a wallet. The subtle requires the subtlest handling. Not only during high holiday festivals but also in everyday life one should beware of rending one's garment. On holidays people care for their clothing, but during routine occupations they are not concerned about it. How many of the subtlest garments go to ruin!

248. Incaution leads to error. Where is the old and where is the new? One needs to be careful.

249. You yourselves see how many people fail to understand the meaning of simple words. At such a level it is necessary to excuse their confused minds and to repeat the words as to a deaf person. Many times, in speaking with the deaf, one is uncertain whether or not many of the words reached their consciousness. It is very difficult to take into consideration all deficiencies of hearing, sight, and the other senses. But go forward, knowing that though few listeners hear, and few see, yet space sees and hears. Thus proceed.

250. You have already observed how, through a certain straining of sight, it is possible to see faces of former incarnations. One may clearly perceive how a face of the present is reconstructed into an image of a past age. Vibrations and crystal formations indicate the presence of a definite energy. There can be no question of autosuggestion, for neither of the persons participating in the experiment know into what the formations are molded. Often the reconstruction begins, not in alteration of the facial lines, but in some details of headdress or clothing. The very character of the face changes quite imperceptibly, and in the most unexpected features. It may be noted that faces rarely hold to their present type. During all such unexpected metamorphoses, all premeditation is precluded. A very painful tension of the eyes indicates that the process is not a mental one, but that psychic energy is acting through the optic centers. Frequent experiences of this nature can injure the sight, yet the presence of such physical clairvoyance is exceedingly important. There can be clairvoyance under suggestion, but then the psychic energy is acting through the brain, and it is always possible to suspect suggestion on the part of the hypnotist himself. It is far more convincing when psychic energy acts directly. The same directness is expressed also in actions with the pendulum of life. Autosuggestion is similarly excluded. An honest investigator does not know the results to be received. He is often more astonished than the others present. In both the first and the second case, onlookers are altogether undesirable. There should be nothing in the vicinity which can influence the psychic energy.

The antiquity of such experiments is incalculable. Besides, they have served in state and judicial matters. It is necessary to recognize the extent of the unique usefulness of such experiments with psychic energy. They provide a barometer of illnesses and disturbances of the spirit, as well as of sincerity itself—and also of obsession.

251. If all the experiments with psychic energy were to be collated, a treasure-trove of access to the Higher World would be at hand. Nothing supernatural or dark should encumber such observations. This research upon the great psychic energy should be natural, honest and useful.

252. The following interpretation of Aum will also be propounded: the first letter—manifested as the basis; the second—manifested in the subtlest energies; the third—the ineffable in fire and grandeur. Each interpretation leads to the same triune structure, from which, as from Truth, one cannot escape.

It is also said that the general significance of the word yes as affirmation is the same. It can be found in all tongues; sometimes it will even resound externally. So let us not be inordinately submerged in explanatory interpretations which have frequently been altered. The chief consideration is that the essence of the concept remain inviolate. Let us invoke all steadfastness.

253. Lack of steadfastness was especially condemned in antiquity. It was called ruination and was regarded with reproach, as the barrier to advancement. Wavering was considered to be ignorance and failure in the primary education. It was assumed that the disciple would not wander away from the true basis, but would continue persistently to perfect himself.

254. The process of self-perfection was not regarded as egoistic. Improvement has the General Welfare as its goal, and by its nature cannot be a personal acquisition; for example, each good thought is universally beneficial in space.

255. In many countries, when people wish to express a steadfast affirmation, they solemnly pronounce the word Amen. The origin of many words can be traced to ancient sources. When we examine the meaning of the word Amen in Greek, Hebrew, Egyptian, and Sumerian, through many steps we arrive at the same affirmation of the triune symbol.

Thus, instead of disunity, knowledge teaches only unification. Only those evil by nature strive toward disparagement and disunity. Each follower of knowledge finds everywhere the golden path to the unity of Grandeur and Light.

256. There are people who specifically hate confirmations and proofs. Such people are really and truly ignorant. It may be asked justly, "Did they ever have a consciousness, or do they spring from the animal state?"

You may often be asked, "Does the consciousness

wear out?" The seed of the spirit is everlasting, the Chalice is filled with accumulations, but the degree of consciousness may fluctuate. The principal reason is indolence in the Subtle World. Such a quality can imprison the seed of the spirit and the Chalice as behind forty locks. Especially subject to such indolence is the weak consciousness, which lives its earthly life without overcoming obstacles and without labor. One can observe how such consciousnesses clutch at the Subtle World; not for two thousand years, but for much longer, would they prefer to be spared a new experience. This is how malevolent deniers come to be born.

257. In the Subtle World it is possible to remain in the lower strata for interims centuries long. One should not be astonished at the resourcefulness of certain people; in their insanity they can contrive much that is impossible for a healthy man. Madness of a special kind is to be found in the Subtle World. Unfailingly the law insists upon the date of incarnation, but the madness of the consciousness may be such that in larger measure only evil can be born. Just as cowardly soldiers cut off their fingers in order to avoid the battle, so do the madmen who dwell in the Subtle World contrive to avoid a summons to the banner of labor. It is impossible to evade the law entirely, but it is possible to conceal oneself temporarily in darkness.

258. If scholars are told of magnetized water, they accept such an expression; but if you speak about enchanted or bewitched water, you will be classed with the ignorant. Whereas, the distinction is only in name, for in essence the same energy is applied.

It is time for science to broaden its horizon, unhampered by casual designations. All the dramas of life arise precisely from denominations. One should accustom oneself from childhood to ascertain the essential nature of things.

259. You know what a great part psychic energy plays in the subtlest manifestations. It is difficult for people to realize that each manifestation of thought leaves a trace which is physically perceptible. Is it not wonderful to follow the outflow of thought in each line of a manuscript? It is not less remarkable to note how one psychic energy evokes the display of another, stratified upon an object. In such a manner one can understand to what a degree the atmosphere, saturated by precipitations of psychic energy, is manifested in the aspect of perceptible crystals. The time will come when the ponderability of thought will be revealed.

260. A great number of painful sensations are caused by psycho-atmospheric tensions. We do not mean atmospheric pressures only, but actual psychic waves, which not only can create moods but can even reflect upon the nerve centers. One cannot imagine to what an extent the atmosphere is saturated by psychic energies; such emanations produce effects not only upon animal life but also upon plants. Therefore, it is impossible light-mindedly to attribute all these manifestations merely to crude physical conditions. Many of the subtlest psychic manifestations still have not been unriddled; for the consciousness itself is often primitive. Many times you have observed such singular incongruities.

261. You have observed that the psychic energy stratified upon an object can be eradicated neither by distance nor by other conditions. This but imposes the greater responsibility on man as the bearer of such power. This was told long ago, but the occult expressions have not enabled people to realize the significance of the force of psychic energy. What right has man to defile the surrounding space with his impure thoughts!

Much should be written about the significance of the basic energy; otherwise, vague and unenlightened thinking will again obscure the source of well-being. One history has not yet been written, namely the history of forgetfulness. Such a chronicle of involution would be useful. Indeed, the study of ancient periods has been made very difficult, for many discoveries await disclosure; yet there exists certain data which is already sufficient to enable humanity to observe many waves of forgetfulness.

262. Objects good and evil are created by man. Good thoughts and benevolent contacts combine to create an object of blessing; and on the other hand, the touches of evil can create a very infectious nidus.

Let us not refer light-mindedly to the essence of psychic energy.

263. During experiments with psychic energy a certain fatigue is inevitable. Such a sensation merely indicates that the energy is actually in operation. It is deplorable to degrade this energy by regarding it as a lower physiological force. It is possible to investigate it in all spheres and to observe its expanse in space. Experiment in the lofty spheres can yield significant results.

264. In the study of the history of faiths it is possible to observe how humanity has repeatedly grasped subtle conceptions only to forget and later cast aside that which had been cognized. One may see how in ancient times people grasped the law of reincarnation only to reject it again in a spasm of rage. The reason for this ecclesiastic denial is understandable—a caste was protecting its prerogatives, for the law of Existence threatened to equalize the rights of people.

So it has happened in different ages, yet the waves of cognition and of ignorance are everywhere identical. They create an agitation of the waters so needed for the advancement of consciousness. Therefore, each one striving for knowledge achieves tranquility of spirit amid storm and stress.

Let us not remain in ignorance when knowledge is knocking at all gates.

265. Knowledge will always be positive and affirmative. There is no time to concern oneself with denials and forbiddances. Unbelief and error are results of ignorance. Knowledge searches, investigates and affirms. When it encounters oppositions, it first of all puts the question, "Is this not something merely illusory? Has not the spectre of contradiction appeared?" Knowledge cannot parry with a spectre, therefore, knowledge first of all investigates amiably the apparent contradictions. Knowledge does not permit dissensions before the face of the Higher World. An exchange of opinions is not a quarrel.

266. There is so much intolerance and brutality in humanity that it is not difficult to arrive at a conclusion as to its degree of ignorance. Such a degree of ignorance forces one to reiterate the fundamentals. Of what avail is man's literacy if he remain only a beast! Animals too have learned to understand certain signs, yet they are still animals eager for bloodshed.

Therefore, it is necessary to tell of the shame of ignorance with special brevity and speed.

267. Each prayer is a beginning and not a conclusion. Ordinarily prayer is understood as something final, whereas there can be no communion with the Higher World without consequences. Each slight opening of the sacred Gates already renews the chords of the consciousness. This renewal does not bespeak the past but is directed into the future. Thus, prayer is the gateway to the future. This creative force should be kept in mind. It is inadmissible to limit oneself to the gesture of outward prayer; such hypocrisy is the most dangerous blasphemy. Yet it is impossible to affirm the power of communion with the Higher World so long as the basic energy remains unrealized. Therefore, knowledge of the Subtle World helps to construct the step to the Higher World. The Subtle World has already become almost a laboratory concept. Though the names be diverse, the goal of the quest is one. Let us not disturb the scholars who draw close to the Great Unknown. We are indifferent as to how they name the sparks of the One Light. In approaching, they will suspect that there are a great number of subdivisions. They will be right from their point of view, because psychic energy reveals its face according to the quality of energy of the investigator.

268. The multiformity of psychic energy is evidence of its power; it cannot remain inert. As true Fire it vibrates and acts incessantly. People may think that their energy is quietly asleep, but in its essential nature it cannot remain inactive owing to its bond with the higher energy.

269. Each one desirous of investigating psychic energy must first of all test his own psychic energy. During different experiments he may observe how his own energy acts. Each energy has particular qualities. It is erroneous to think that, since the law is one, all partial manifestations will be completely identical.

The more subtle the energy, the more indistinguishable to the crude vision will be its qualities. Thus, it is necessary first of all to establish firmly the basic quality, which is the touchstone. This quality is purity of thoughts, arising from desire toward unselfish usefulness. The rays of achievement will be the best torches during the study of psychic energy. Attentiveness also will be a friend in such experiments. Any foregone conclusion will be detrimental.

Psychic energy is precipitated upon all objects. Its sediments correspond to the precipitations of space, therefore it is possible to study not only the state of a personal energy but also that of the collective energy. For this it is necessary to experiment with snow or rain water. In the general course of observations many new combinations will be produced.

270. Help from the Subtle World and the Higher World is also useful for experiments. Pure thinking will be an immediate guarantee of cooperation. No invocations are needed, for the consonance of the heart already creates a bridge of light. Thus, in everything it is possible to find the greatest usefulness. A single thought about psychic energy will bestow opportunity for broadening the consciousness.

271. Perceptivity is a special quality of the consciousness. It does not depend upon the intellect; it does not depend upon surroundings; it does not depend upon the schooling—it is formed in the domain of the heart. The man who has accumulated this quality cannot be deprived of perception. By means of psychic energy he finds opportunity for observation even among the most adverse circumstances.

It is especially significant to observe such people from childhood. They differ distinctly from those around them, and they seem to know their destiny. Sometimes this knowledge is revealed by unexpected words. Sometimes the very actions of a child show how eagerly his spirit is seeking some definite goal, but usually such strivings are misunderstood. This sacred peculiarity of one summoned to ascent is much ridiculed. But in the future epoch it is the ones excelling in perceptivity who will be particularly esteemed.

272. It is vain for someone to affirm that the invisible world does not exist, such a falsehood is equivalent to denying the existence of thought. Thought also is invisible, but only ignorance denies the mental process. Accordingly, it would be possible to begin the rejection of all energies, for they too are invisible. Besides, is the unseen world invisible for all? Let the deniers not judge by themselves. Judging by oneself creates a hotbed of egoism.

273. It may seem that the Teaching is given in one dimension, but by tracing the sequence of the Teaching one can see the turns of an ascending spiral. Such curving is effected in order that humanity be imperceptibly moved forward. Just as we cannot perceive the extent of growth of grass each instant, so, too, the new turn of the spiral does not register in the consciousness. Human reason cannot contain the fiery structure; hence, one should goal-fittingly give to it as much as it can absorb. The consequences of incommensurateness are monstrous, and one must not thrust a monstrosity upon the world through one's own ignorance. The structure must be harmonious. Therefore, it is instructive to compare the steps provided by the Teaching; thus is obtained a significant ladder of ascent.

274. If a man says, "I have done all within my power," do not believe him. He is excusing himself, while at the same time setting limitations. When a man imagines that all has been exhausted, precisely then he loses the key to the saving gateway. Often through ignorance or indolence people renounce the best solutions. How often have We spoken about the inexhaustibility of heart energy, but man himself can

bury it and deprive himself of the best possibility. By its very nature a statement that all forces have been exhausted is conceited. Is it not self-pity that suggests giving up and washing one's hands of a situation? Often man pities himself and closes the access to Higher Forces.

When people will realize the correlation of energies, they will discover the stronghold of their own invincibility.

275. It is right that you turn your attention to the blows repelled by the aura. Only a few realize such mental assaults. People usually attribute such manifestations to accidental physical causes, but the developed consciousness, even during sleep, will determine the true cause. The consciousness is a faithful shield. The aura and the consciousness form a protective armor.

276. People ordinarily avoid the word unity; they are afraid of it. At the same time they talk much about sympathy, but they forget that these concepts are identical—one without the other is unthinkable. Likewise with other concepts; people try to accept the one carrying the least responsibility. Sympathy may be limited to words, but unity necessitates action. Each action is in itself frightening to cowards. They do not wish to understand that each thought of sympathy is a powerful action, if the thought is suitably expressed. Often sympathy is limited to empty sounds. In such a case neither creative thought nor action takes place. A lack of thought kills sympathy, and inaction dissolves unity. Man fears responsibility, and with this he falls into heartlessness.

277. The particles of higher energy which exist in each human organism correspondingly exist in the other kingdoms of nature. The animal kingdom and the vegetable kingdom know how to preserve the par-

ticle of energy also in the Subtle World. Especially certain animals that lived around man preserve a certain bond with the organism of the Subtle World dweller. When I advise kindness toward animals, I have in mind that it is better to encounter small friends than enemies. Indeed, one should preserve co-measurement in everything, otherwise one may receive harmful emanations from animals.

Likewise, when I indicate a vegetable diet, I am guarding against nourishing the subtle body with blood. The essence of blood thoroughly permeates the body and even the subtle body. Blood is so undesirable in the diet that only in extreme cases do We permit the use of meat which has been dried in the sun. It is also possible to use those parts of the animal where the blood substance has been thoroughly transmuted. Thus, vegetable food has a significance also for life in the Subtle World.

278. It is often asked, "Do animals retain their appearance in the Subtle World?" Rarely, because the absence of consciousness renders them formless; sometimes there are foggy outlines, like impulses of energy, but most often they are imperceptible. In fact, the manifestation of animals pertains to the lower strata of the Subtle World. Such obscurities can terrify one by their confused appearance. I consider that the subtle body of man should not remain in these strata, but in their consciousness people frequently resemble animals.

279. The Subtle World is filled with prototypes of animals, but only a strong consciousness perceives them. Indeed, the aspects of such animal representatives are innumerable, from the most complicated to those which are decomposing as dross. It should not be thought that the dwellers of the Subtle World all possess identical vision.

Good clear sight is due to clarity of consciousness, therefore from beginning to end We advise showing care in the matter of clear consciousness. Long ago it was said that good does not dwell in a muddy well.

280. One can observe the extent to which there simultaneously dwell on Earth living beings of the most diverse status—from primitive savage to subtlest thinker. One person will assert that Earth is in the Paleolithic period, whereas another will demonstrate that Earth has already entered the Golden Age, each will be guided by what is evident to him. So, too, in the cosmogonic discussions one should not be astonished at the contiguity of quite different periods. The Universe is so multiform in its great Infinity.

281. The psychic energy of a crowd must be observed. Here it is possible to ascertain the increment of force in a direct ratio; actually, where two are united in thought the result is the force of three. But it should not be forgotten that each counteracting thought consumes much surrounding energy; that is why it is so rarely possible to observe a successful unity. Truly, a single horse can hold back the entire caravan and defeat a successful consummation. Again will be woven a fabric of the best energies, but humanity will prodigally squander the ordained attainments. It is so easy to arrive at an understanding of the value of unified energies. This is not an abstraction but an actual physical reality.

People wish to conquer and appropriate everything, yet for them the power of thought is idle dreaming! Thus are true treasures dissipated.

282. The liar is always convinced that his lie will remain undetected. The murderer believes that his crime will remain secret. Sometimes one may hear that suggestion and psychic energy are utilized in the law court, but such attempts remain isolated, and no realization is aroused of the natural possibilities of the struggle with evil.

283. Evil should be opposed, as a manifestation of chaos. Entire countries protect themselves against the ocean, which would otherwise inundate them forever. The unified labors of the whole nation construct imposing ramparts of protection. So, too, chaos can engulf the entire wealth of a people. It should be understood that the waves of chaos are penetrating the consciousness of mankind. Evolution is the antipode of chaos. Let us not be deaf to the rumblings of chaos!

284. With difficulty do people dare to pronounce the simplest law: "Blessed are the obstacles, by them we grow." Tests are admitted easily enough, as long as they have not begun. No one is willing to quicken his progress through obstacles.

Yet it is still more intolerable to humanity to hear of the usefulness of suffering. The reason is not fear of pain or discomfort, but that people fail to cognize a life transcending earthly existence. They are ready to suffer the discomfort of any night-lodging for the sake of tomorrow's festival, but they are unwilling to co-measure earthly life with Infinity.

Of all actions manifested by a thinking being, terror before Infinity is the most impermissibly degrading.

285. Where can there be thought of Infinity, if man limits himself to an earthly existence? No one helps the child to look joyfully into the future; that is why labor has been conceived as a curse. True, the life span of people has been extended, but what significance has such extension if men persist in ignoring the grandeur of Infinity!

286. Another limitation which hampers the ascent of man is his failure to pay attention to what takes place close around him. He wants that which belongs to another; he is impressed only by something alien; yet the closest and most precious attracts no attention and provokes no study. Such incommensurateness is the result of ignorance. One must apply judicious observation to everything. Such a state of affairs is quite usual, but the developed consciousness must correct such limited thinking.

287. Psychology is the science of mind. The study of thought cannot be confined to one people or to a single stratum of a people. The comparison of consciousnesses of different nations will yield surprising deductions. One can observe how independent of external civilization is the potential of thought. Likewise one may convince oneself that wealth will not go hand in hand with thought. Apparently the most onerous conditions contribute to a deepening of thought. Lack of means favors refinement of consciousness.

History shows how the nests of true thoughts have been put together, therefore the science of thought is the science of Be-ness. It is inadmissible to complicate the study of thought with any restrictions. Besides, this science must be forever alive, for thought continually vibrates and lives in space. Thus, an aspiring study of thought leads to an understanding of so-called phenomena, which are nothing but unrealized psychic energy in its various manifestations.

288. Completely inadmissible are malevolent prayers and self-pity. When a man cries out—Why?—he is thinking neither of the past nor the future. He isolates himself from the Higher Forces, as if accusing Them. Likewise, woe to the man who importunes the Higher Forces to harm others. Both conceit and ignorance resound when a man, instead of merging with the Higher Forces, tries to set Them on a path of hatred and cruelty.

289. There have been the strangest attempts to study the transmissions of thought at a distance. People have connected two persons at a distance by tying their wrists with a thread of waxed silk. They paid special attention to the purity of the silk and the particular quality of the wax. They gave much thought to how best to insulate the thread from the ground. But they were far from remembering that psychic energy needs neither thread nor wax. People deem that the mechanical appliance actually effects the success, but he who first proposed this method regarded the thread simply as a symbol on which to concentrate attention.

290. Since transmission of thought at a distance exists, then the interception of such thoughts in space must also be possible. Indeed, one should carefully remember this circumstance. Besides the intrusion of extraneous thoughts, in both the earthly and Subtle Worlds, special circumstances are possible, which contribute to the interception of thoughts. Uniformity of auras can facilitate the admission of thoughts; when people have lived long together or have corresponded, they can be involved in a current. If such people become dangerous, it is necessary to break the bond of the auras. Such an action must not be instantaneous, otherwise it will react upon the health. Each such process must take place naturally.

291. Decidedly, all unbalanced conditions must be eliminated naturally. Each passionate unbalance cannot be arrested by command or by compulsion. Striving will build a firm bridge on the foundation of a refined consciousness. One must recognize the usefulness, and then comes true evolution. But without realization it is impossible to overcome the lower earthly passions.

The sphere surrounding Earth is dense with humanity's passions. No external forces will disperse this fog fabricated by humanity itself. Therefore, consonance and color and the best thoughts provide the antitoxin against the infection of chaos.

292. In a time of especially pressing currents, the Teacher must remind about all the circumstances which need counteraction. One should not regard such repetition of reminders as allusions to forgetfulness; on the contrary, they are only a fortification, when a complexity of events dims, as it were, the clarity of the path.

The complexity of events is a collision of the manifest with chaos, or of Light with darkness. During such a tremendous conflict a great number of transitional steps are apparent, therefore the perplexities of those who cannot clearly discern the subtlest deviations are comprehensible. Around the rainbow are many varied refractions.

293. If the precipitates of space upon cities were to be investigated, something similar to imperil would be found among the poisonous substances. Carefully observing this poison, one comes to the conviction that it is imperil exhaled by the breath of evil. Undoubtedly, breathing permeated with evil is a carrier of injurious effects. If poison can be deposited in the organism, due to irritation, if the saliva can be made poisonous, then the breath can also be made a poison-carrier. It is necessary to judge how much evil is being exhaled and how multiform are the aspects of evil compressed into the new combinations of poisons present in enormous crowds of people. This is increased by the varied effluvia of decomposing foods and all manner of refuse which litter the streets even in metropolises. It is time to look after the cleanliness of backyards. Cleanliness is necessary out of doors and in the human breathing. The imperil exhaled by irritated people is identical with filth, or shameful refuse. It is imperative to impress people's consciousness with the fact that each bit of filth infects those around. The filth of moral dissolution is worse than any excretions.

294. Nothing can vindicate the self-generation of poison, it is the equivalent of murder and suicide. Even the most undeveloped people sense the approach of such a poison-bearer. Distress, anxiety and fear enter with him. Many physical diseases break out as a result of the infiltration of imperil—just as if a firebrand had worked its way in.

295. The speed of thought transmission at a distance is incredible. But conditions exist which retard even this lightning-speed energy, namely an atmosphere poisoned by imperil. Observations upon thought can yield remarkable deductions pertaining to both the physical and the psychic. One can see how evil thought engenders imperil, a physical substance; the same substance is also involved in psychic transmission, and can even retard the speedy reception of the sending. Thus, imperil can progressively complicate the effects of thoughts. Pay attention to the fact that imperil is born of egoism, but that it acts beyond self upon broad masses. This means that egoism is criminal not only as regards the egoist himself but also in relation to people at large.

Many of the most useful observations are made during experiments with thought. Precisely such reflections constitute the opposition to egoism. Each suffering is already an advancement.

296. Many primitive methods for recalling events

to mind may be observed. One may read how one ruler inclined his head as far as his knees, that the change in the blood circulation might help to awaken his sleeping memory. It is known that anchorites beat their breasts in order to stimulate the chalice. The evidence of many examples demonstrates that blood circulation is connected with psychic functions. The more necessary it is to respect the science that examines the physical side of life, but at the same time reveals a new spiritual bond inherent in all Existence.

297. A good instrument easily displays new qualities under every test. Truly, anything of good quality fears no test. Each test teaches new conditions which might otherwise remain unnoticed. Whoever fears testing is an ignorant coward. When a man is ready in heart to undergo all of life's experiences, he can think about advancement; he can distinguish between harm and usefulness.

What joy it is to devote oneself to the Common Good, not abstractly but in conscious advancement!

298. We often mention physicians and scientists, but it must not be thought that other occupations should not also be mentioned in speaking of the Higher World. Can lawyers and judges administer earthly laws if they have no concept of the laws of the Universe? How can they establish earthly law without thinking of universal justice? It is impossible to isolate Earth from all the worlds; it is necessary to understand the interaction of the earthly world and the Subtle World in order to acquire the right to judge people's conduct. It is wrong to restrict oneself to former casual decisions which do not conform to present conditions. Each time has its own peculiarities, and without a clear picture of the evolutionary situation the court will err.

Verily, the judge takes upon himself a great responsibility if he is to remain at the helm of universal justice.

299. Likewise, architects must be enriched with inspiration from the treasuries of universal cognition. The style of a period is molded out of life, winged by knowledge. How superb are the structures into which the thought of beauty has been impressed! One can see the ascent of entire epochs through their constructive inspiration. The very quality of the structures is felt in the strength of their materials. The builder must also know the material which endures. Can he deny the Higher World?

300. It is superfluous to speak of the meaning of striving to the Higher World to poets, musicians, artists, sculptors, and singers, because their expression of beauty is founded on inspiration. Who, then, can define the boundary between inspiration and Hiero-inspiration? Such a boundary line between inspirations is undefinable. Each inspiration contains some particle of Hiero-inspiration. Only the heart itself can determine the degree of its exaltation. The true participant of beauty can sense the Guiding Principle brooding above earthly expression. Therefore, there is no need to convince the servitors of beauty of its lofty heights.

He is no sower in the field of creation who feels no tremor in the realization that he creates beauty.

301. Nor can any of the other domains of human labor disown the Higher Principle. If the tiller of the soil is only a daily slave, his labor will never expand. Each form of work has a creative domain. Earthly thought binds one within earthly limits, but evolution contains the Higher Principle.

Books should be written on the different domains of labor. Therein servile, circumscribed toil should be compared with unbounded creative labor. It is necessary to demonstrate in a strictly scientific manner the possibilities which can be reached through a regeneration of the quality of labor. People who are depressed by the daily routine lose sight of the horizon. So, too, the eyes of man cannot at once become accustomed to the light. Let science in all ways aid the expansion of the horizon.

302. One can observe in the details of life how many cosmic waves touch Earth. Only the ignorant can deny the frequency with which great currents penetrate space. Events can be foretold, but it is significant also to follow the connection of events with psychic and physical manifestations. Without astrology, by the observation of nature alone, it is possible to compare physical manifestations with current events.

Humanity creates more than people think.

303. Man should be told, "Do not weaken yourself; discontent, doubt, self-pity, all consume the psychic energy." The manifestation of enshrouded toil—what a frightful spectacle! One should compare the fruits of luminous labor with those of a toil enshrouded by man when he has robbed himself.

I deem that science should also aid in this procedure. Apparatus already exist for the measuring of blood pressure; there will also be apparatus for comparing the organism in its overburdened or inspired state. It can be proven that a man who is unmolested by the influence of the three vipers mentioned above works ten times better; besides, he preserves an immunity against all illnesses. Thus, again it is possible to be convinced graphically that the psychic principle prevails over the physical.

It is evident, especially at present, how much harm humanity is inflicting upon itself. Each thought is either a stone in the construction or poison in the heart. It need not be thought that, when speaking about self-poisoning, We have in mind anything new—this truth is as old as the world! But when the vessel is approaching shipwreck, all forces should be summoned to the common task.

304. Earthly cares are like stones rolling down a mountain. The lower down they roll, the more violent the impact of the landslide. Would it not be better to ascend to the very summit where there are no falling stones? Upward striving also transforms our attitude toward earthly cares. Even though they continue, their meaning is altered.

Thus one may perceive how many advantages the summit has over the canyon.

305. Obsession and self-poisoning are close companions. They are equally little recognized by people. During the process of self-poisoning, obsession is especially easy, but under obsession poisoning ultimately takes place; such poisoning is ineradicable. Certain people assert that during obsession the health not only does not fail but even improves. This is a great error, the apparent good health is the result of the nervous tension only. Moreover, the intrusion of a foreign psychic energy inevitably opens a channel to various infections. Obsession is not psychism, but it affects the entire organism. Let us say definitely—obsession is not only a psychic sickness but also an evidence of infection of the whole organism. Many epidemics have obsession as their origin. Indeed, the dark obsessing entity is not concerned about the health of its victim. Every disease is in itself a dissolution which is pleasing to darkness. Two psychic energies cannot live long together. Periodically there may be a relaxation of the obsession, such a method is employed by the obsessors if they value the victim.

306. Aspiration toward the Higher World is the best recourse against obsession. Thinking about the Higher World is the best proven antitoxin. Exalted thoughts not only influence the nerve substance, but also purify the blood. Experiments with the composition of the blood in relation to the thinking of the patient are highly instructive.

307. Truly, the atmosphere is heavy. Noticeable to Us is the condensation of the lower strata around Earth. The causes are many, but it is impossible that the battle be without consequences. All the more imperative is care of the health, in fact, great care about everything is needed.

When I speak of unity, I have in mind not only a spiritual necessity but also physical health. People prefer not to know about the latter, and afterwards bewail the grievous results.

308. At times during a convalescence, one may observe that something impedes the process. It may be surmised that the patient himself is retarding the efforts of the organism by a negative attitude, but it is possible to be convinced that other causes exist outside of man's sphere of influence. Spatial currents can be strong determinants of any reaction. In hospitals, where observations upon many individuals are possible, there should be expert observation of the causes of different effects of the same medicine. Many clues for this may be found in spatial conditions. It should not be thought that a clear blue sky is necessarily an indicator of useful currents; it may be that a threatening, clouded sky carries better currents.

Seldom observed are the spatial currents, and slight attention is paid to varying human moods. It is impossible to explain everything as caused by the thoughts which permeate space. Besides, there exist the subtlest chemisms of the remote worlds; such currents come into contact with the lower, supra-earthly strata. One may imagine what combinations result! In this case also, man is too indifferent to his neighbor.

309. Follow the development of science for the last half-century; the progress of knowledge is amazing. Schools should give graphic demonstrations of science, as it was fifty years ago, and as it is today. Such a striking comparison can open man's eyes to the possibilities of the future. No one should be so benighted as to forbid the development of knowledge. He is not of man's calibre who persecutes science! Let us repeat this indictment without end, as long as this shagginess of thought remains unmortified.

Such a reminder is even more timely since science, despite its speedy growth, has not accomplished a tenth of what was ordained for it during this period. Much of this must be ascribed to the inertia of humanity. But for all that, it is distressing to see that the most advanced of scientists are not appreciated. People wish to investigate space; modest stratosphere excursions, telescopic observations, the study of the luminaries— all revolve within a vicious circle, because psychic energy is unrecognized. Without it, the boldest flight remains a childish diversion. Without psychic energy, the pathways of space will be difficult to discern.

The same thing takes place in all domains of science. It is utterly senseless to disregard the higher energy. As during religious wars and persecutions, those with daring and acute perceptions must, like alchemists of old, hide from inquisition. Such a disgraceful situation is not to be tolerated.

310. Nor is a reminder about inquisition to be considered out of place. Unfortunately, it is applicable to many things. Various aspects of life are under inquisitional pressure. Indeed, this dark principle weakens the best undertakings. Darkness makes its nest in mansions as well as in hovels.

Let us not lull ourselves with the idea that certain minds will solve the problems for everyone. Humanity is obliged to think; it must strive unitedly for attainments. One cannot allow the chaos of ignorance, gaudily attired, to crash in and jeer at knowledge.

311. Stations are established in various countries to investigate atmospheric conditions. In fact, meteorological observations in widely remote countries have much significance.

With equal precision should observations upon the manifestations of psychic energy in different countries be coordinated. It may be observed that at times in the most remote lands simultaneous surgings of spirit flash out like reflections of some higher causes. Similarly, simultaneous depressions of spirit may be expressed among the most diverse people. Such mass manifestations must be studied. But there are no institutes to undertake such an important task. Perhaps individual observers may be found who realize the importance of such comparisons, but their efforts, being uncoordinated, generally founder in confusion and doubt. There appear to exist societies consecrated to the higher wisdom, but they have no scientific sections.

There should be cooperation among all nations for the careful observation and comparison of manifestations of psychic energy. The universality of observation would demonstrate the unity of the higher energy. Only by such observation is it possible naturally to obtain a clear conception of the Higher World.

What dialect, what words, can transmit to people an understanding of their true progress!

312. It is a terrifying time indeed, yet the majority of people do not sense its causes. With a blare of all trumpets one should proclaim—Armageddon! Yet people will merely ask, "What price is a pound of Armageddon?" There has never been such a confusion of the trivial and the great. It would be better if, when people do not understand, they would at least desist from interfering in the Battle, but their obstructions make the most direct paths tortuous.

313. There is much ingratitude. I advise you in the future to lay up a store of patience against ingratitude and ignorance. Strangers are often more thoughtful, therefore We classify people first of all on the basis of gratitude.

314. Everyone may observe evidences of psychic energy in any place and at any time. One needs to concentrate attention and, however briefly, to note the observed manifestations. Certainly among these notes some may be useless, but this should not disturb one. Written notes have an enormous significance, because manifestations of psychic energy are forgotten with extraordinary speed. Each day something unusual takes place. It should not be considered that only striking manifestations have significance, sometimes the grasping of a thought or the discovery of some needed pages may offer a very significant example of the working of psychic energy. Besides, the path of attention also produces patience, an indispensable quality for the investigator.

315. You have a wide correspondence with various countries. If your friends begin to record such notes about psychic energy, an important comparison can be made, not only of the facts themselves but also of

the individual attitude toward them. Likewise, climatic conditions and local events necessarily infuse a characteristic note. The entire variation of conditions of life can be observed by means of such writings. The steadfastness of unwavering attention helps to deepen observations.

316. Correct is the thought to note down the different regulations and institutions useful to humanity. Evolution requires new forms in everything. Useful deductions should be discovered in already crystallized circumstances. The limits of knowledge are expanding. New interrelations are being created between the branches of science. Much which once appeared separate is now proved to issue from a single root. A need for new cooperative combinations is evident. It is imperative to study former subdivisions, replacing them with more goal-fitted ones. Such a need exists in all the domains of life—from philosophy and creed to the most practical sciences.

In using the word practical, I speak not literally but merely to apply the accepted expression. Of course efficacy is far removed from so-called practicality. The ability to discern how greatly efficacy outruns the mechanistic conception of life enables one to understand how great a regeneration humanity needs for evolution.

One should not be distressed because certain needed institutions may not find recognition at once. Let thought continue to work. People do not keep pace with the flight of thought, yet none the less thought leads the world.

317. One may ask, "What is the connection between Aum and useful institutions?" Both are expressions of harmony; thus, lofty concepts cannot be separated. Only prejudice is so blind as not to see the paths to unity.

318. Sometimes people reach such a limited state that they manage to reduce everything to insignificance. The very loftiest communion is for them grist to the mill! Striving becomes weakened by all kinds of superstitions. Such infection makes its nest in the most diverse people.

It has been said of the Middle or Golden Way, "It is better to call it a Path, so narrow is the passage between monsters."

319. Many dragons stand guard to impede each advance. Multi-colored are these monsters! Among the most repulsive is the drab dragon of everyday routine. It would make an empty gray cobweb of even the most lofty communion. Yet even in everyday life people know how to preserve the freshness of renewal. People wash themselves daily and find themselves refreshed before the next task. Likewise, spiritual ablutions should not become dusty drudgery. Few know how to overcome the dragon of everyday routine. But such heroes multiply their forces tenfold, and each day they raise their eyes anew unto the heavens.

Since Infinity is, the spirit of man has no single commonplace instant. Joy can be born of a uniqueness of sensation. But lofty communion cannot become something ordinary. Boredom is not in Infinity, but in human limitations.

Do not permit the gray dragon to triumph. It is not really strong, and its repulsiveness is only in the ugliness of habit. Where filth and ugliness have been eliminated, the gray dragon cannot exist. Thus, the conquest of daily routine is reverence of the Higher World.

320. Whoever loves precise knowledge must know

how to receive it. Many talk of their devotion to precise knowledge, but in practice they clothe each fact in the motley rags of prejudice. They do not sense the unreality of their own premises. They bewail the inadequacy of material for observation, yet at the same time disregard the most unprecedented events. They would revolve the Universe according to the digestive state of their own stomach. They reject the most apparent manifestation if it does not conform to their mood. But can such be the path of precise knowledge? Where then is patience? Where good will? Where tirelessness? Where observation? Where attentiveness, which opens the gates?

Let us not weary of repeating how readily all gates open in the absence of complaints, discontent, and negation.

321. Sandstorms are sources of infection. One should observe where the waves of these frightful destroyers are passing. It is far from useful to permit such destructions. People may justly condemn those who have permitted the destruction of life. For entire ages people have helped to fill the lower strata of the atmosphere with particles of decomposition.

Is it not time to reflect on the relationship of psychic energy to the surrounding atmospheric strata? It is not permissible to poison the psychic energy of entire generations! So many beautiful souls perish, because of the poisoning of the planet!

322. The rhythm of labor is the adornment of the world. Labor may be regarded as a victory over everyday routine. Each hard-working man is a benefactor of humanity. To imagine Earth without workers is to see a reversion to chaos. Invincible tenacity is forged by labor; precisely everyday work is the accumulation of the treasure. The true toiler loves his labor and understands the significance of tension.

Work has already been called prayer. The highest unity and quality of labor arises from its rhythm. The best quality of work brings forth the rhythm of the Beautiful. Each labor contains within itself the concept of the Beautiful.

Labor, prayer, beauty—all are facets of the great crystal of Existence.

323. After labor the worker is better and more tolerant. A great deal of perfecting takes place in work. In toil lies evolution!

324. The creation of good should be so natural an occupation of man that it should not be necessary to speak of this goal. Man cannot point to his good deeds as something exceptional; otherwise it could be presumed that man's usual state is evil, and that only by exception does he at times arrive at something good.

Many errors have been accumulated in the course of thousands of years. People began to measure good by a gold standard. Men, carrying gold and precious stones into the temple, assured themselves that these represented the world's best attainments. People filled themselves with false concepts about treasures; they remembered the legend about gold as the source of evil, but they hastened to transform it into a fairy tale. The history of mankind reveals repeated revolts against gold. Each great Teacher has manifested himself an insurgent against gold, and people have hastened to kill each daring rebel against their cherished idol. Indeed, I do not speak of a lump of gold itself but of the entire horror which surrounds it.

325. Among secret things, especially undiscoverable remains the knowledge as to who reaps the most benefit from the good sent forth. No one knows whom his goodness has helped. It may be assumed that a thought of good reaches a definite person, but this is only a supposition. It may be that this thought has greatly aided someone unknown to us. Such a thought is a messenger of good, and the rescued man may not know his savior; so his gratitude is turned toward the Higher World. When he wishes to express his enraptured gratefulness, he looks upward into the eternal Furnace of Creative Thought.

326. Anonymous thoughts also receive secret gratitude. Each thought of good receives the best gratitude. It is not for us to judge where the song of gratitude will arise. There is no need to get ahead of words of gratitude; the most beautiful song of gratitude resounds in a moment of joy. But then, the thought of such joy has been sent by someone.

Let us say gratefully—Aum!

327. If, after perusal of all books about the Good, a man does not learn patience, containment and co-measurement, he is no man. From such hard hearts no gratitude resounds. I often reiterate in different symbols about the quality of gratitude. It is imperative to understand the quality of gratitude—it is the adamant of Existence.

328. The world is upheld by Mystery. All Teachings speak about Mystery, the Sacred. At the same time it has been said that there is no secret which would not be revealed. Those who love to seek contradictions may exult; to them it seems that the irreconcilable has been discovered. But they will be judging from an earthly point of view, and, of course, everything super-earthly seems to them illogical. However, apply the same words to the Subtle World and the Higher World, and the earthly contradictions will find their explanation. Indeed, everything that is secretly performed on Earth is already revealed on the higher plane, and the inaccessible Mystery proves logical on the plane of Infinity.

One should know how to estimate earthly contradictions; they arise merely from a limited state of mind. As soon as the higher worlds are actually cognized, the earthly inconsistencies are immediately resolved.

329. It is a pity that at graduation from high school a useful test, applied in olden times, is now omitted. The students had to expound a thesis, selected by themselves, before the most diverse listeners. This required that expressions be found that were comprehensible to all; the task was difficult. For some the students had to find simple words, and yet avoid boring the more educated listeners. Although the gathering was not always satisfied, nevertheless the students applied their best efforts to make themselves understood and, at the same time, touch upon complex and lofty concepts. Such exercises are always useful.

330. One must especially beware of committing an injustice; from it grows ugliness. Man should understand where injustice begins. Not by words is it defined, but by the heart.

331. In anger and irritation man considers himself strong—this is according to earthly considerations. But regarded from the Subtle World, the irritated man is especially powerless. He attracts to himself a great number of small entities which feed on the emanations of anger. Besides, he lets down his own bars and allows even the lower beings to read his thoughts. Therefore, the state of irritation is inadmissible not only as a producer of imperil but also as a gateway for lower entities.

Certainly each irritated person readily agrees with this explanation, but he immediately succumbs to still greater irritation—such is the nature of the ordinary human being. It is amazing how easily they agree, only the more easily to yield again. For this they will invent extraordinary justifications. It may be that the Higher World itself seems guilty in the disordered consciousness of the superficial earth-dweller! It is astonishing to observe people placing the blame for all their own offenses on the Higher World!

Thus one can see that the simplest truths are in need of constant repetition.

332. One cannot condemn those manifestations of which the causes are unknown. Only cognizance of the manifestations of the Subtle World can broaden one's judgment. It is good to recall the parable of the blind man, who, receiving a blow from an elephant's trunk, believed he had been struck by the Hand of God.

Let us refer to the Higher World with all respect.

333. How to fix the boundary between indignation and irritation, or between shock and fear? No one finds words to differentiate such feelings which are almost alike. But the time will come when science will discover the means of analyzing the substance secreted during each emotion. Upon a purely chemical basis it will be determined where and when a definite feeling begins.

The pendulum of life shows by its motion the variation of psychic energy. Just as precisely will the chemism of feelings be determined. The manifestation of the fluctuations of psychic energy shows how continuously vibration goes on, and how it records even the small deviations of energy. So, too, the chemism of feelings cannot be constant. In the microcosm of man it can be observed how intensified are the manifestations of cosmic vibrations. It should not be thought that all these observations are unnecessary; on the contrary, does not perception of the nature of man lead toward the perfection of mankind?

334. I entrust the Teaching to each one who lives in all the worlds. Do not consider such a definition inapplicable. Man actually lives in all the worlds. Each day he visits the worlds, but he cannot be conscious of these momentary absences. Only a few apprehend the sensation of being absent. No extended time is required for the spirit, which exists outside of time. Such sensations are quite characteristic for developed consciousnesses.

335. At times the pendulum of life can be quite inactive. Such signs will be present around paralysis due to evil. Not accidental is the expression, "He choked with malice." Thus it has been shown that malice is limited. The current of malice is not infinite. But it is necessary to observe the fluctuations of the vibrations of energy.

336. Any denial of Truth is ignorant and harmful not only for the denier himself but also spatially. Antagonism to Truth infects space, but there is still more loathsome action when people, after having once realized Truth, later shrink from it. Such a retreat into darkness is madness!

It is possible to find periods in the history of humanity when, after particles of the Truth had been already grasped, certain pseudo-teachers, because of extreme ignorance, tried to again conceal from people the immutable position of things; this resulted in what will some time be regarded as shameful pages of history. The usurpers offered no proofs, but commanded that the obvious be denied. It is as if denial of the sun's existence were prescribed, because someone weak of eyesight could not look at the sun! Similarly prohibited was cognizance of the laws of the Subtle World.

Some, ignorant of them, through egoism forbade others to know the reality.

Let people remember how many recessions into darkness have taken place in different ages. Perhaps such recollections will move humanity toward justice and honesty.

337. Among school studies of history and of comparative religion, let there not be forgotten the various contradictory decisions and enactments of conventions, councils and legislative bodies. Not for confusion of minds is it necessary to know the Truth, but for the reinforcement of the future path. Perfectment rests upon a basis of knowledge.

No one should command a person not to know the Truth and not to strive toward it.

338. If, at times, errors have been made through ignorance or malice, still one cannot tutor entire generations in the same mistakes. People talk much about prejudices, but they are ready to stifle the young generation with requirements that have no meaning.

From everyday routine to cosmogony you find a great number of baseless affirmations not confirmed by experiment and observation.

Constriction of thinking is a gross offense.

339. Each discharge of secretions, each exhalation sends out emanations of psychic energy. Each man lavishly saturates space; therefore he is obligated to show concern about a better quality of psychic energy. If people would understand that each breath has a significance for space, they would take care to purify their breathing. With the simplest apparatus the emanations of psychic energy can be demonstrated. One can see in the swings of the pendulum of life how continuously the energy vibrates. The same means shows the radiations called the aura, which indicates that

particles of the aura are being sent out ceaselessly into space, and psychic energy continually weaves a new protective net.

He who speaks about the inconclusiveness of experiments with psychic energy will usually be one who does not ponder at all about its existence. Dense ignorance contributes to the poisoning of the atmosphere. This must be understood in its literal meaning. Pure breathing is not attained by means of medicines.

Psychic energy is the basis of purifying the breathing.

340. Many of the most beautiful concepts have been perverted. All-forgiveness resounds beautifully, but people have contrived to make it into the monstrous form, "The Higher Forces forgive all," thus making all crimes permissible. However, the matter lies not in forgiveness, which is quite possible, but in living through the consequences. Just is the law of spatial healing. An inflicted wound requires medical treatment. Self-cure requires time, because the torn tissue must be mended. The best consonance of Aum can contribute to the healing of the tissue. But all the consonances of color and aroma can be of help, only if psychic energy admits such cooperation.

341. The conflict with ignorance must be a worldwide manifestation. Not a single nation can boast that it is sufficiently enlightened. No one can find sufficient strength to overcome ignorance in single combat. Knowledge must be universal and upheld in full cooperation. The paths of communication know no barriers; so, too, the paths of knowledge must blossom in the exchange of ideas.

It should not be thought that somewhere enough has been done for education. Knowledge is so much an expanding process that continual renovation of methods is required. It is frightful to see petrified brains which do not admit new attainments! No one inclined to negation can be called a scientist. Science is free, honest, and fearless. Science can instantly alter and elucidate the problems of the Universe. Science is beautiful and therefore infinite. Science cannot stand prohibitions, prejudices, and superstitions. Science can find the great even in quests of the small. Inquire of great scientists how many times the most stupendous discoveries have been made in the process of routine observations. The eye was open, and the brain not dust laden.

The path of those who know how to investigate freely will be the path of the future. Actually, the battle with ignorance is as indeferrable as that with dissolution and corruption. Not easy is the battle with dark ignorance; it has many allies; it is sheltered in many countries; and is covered with different garments. One needs to be supplied with both courage and patience, for the battle with ignorance is a battle with chaos.

342. Experiments upon psychic energy can be carried out in different surroundings and at different times. Dim light sometimes even promotes the manifestation of the energy, but bright sunlight can complicate an experiment by its own strong chemism. There may also be diversity in the conditions of the premises. Best of all is a room which has been permeated with the radiations of the investigator. Yet each casual object can produce its reaction. One should not keep the objects of observation together, especially during the experiment. Likewise, one should not have around resonant objects and string instruments, which can vibrate to irrelevant activations. The very mood of the observer has a great significance. Irritation and unrest can be of no assistance to useful investigation.

When you feel weariness, you should not strain the energy. This force should be guarded under all circumstances. One should not dissipate but conserve the force which miraculously broadens the domain of cognition.

343. Objects surrounding the experiments have more than once astonished those beginning to study. Sometimes the most everyday object has aided the experiment, while another, introduced after extremely thoughtful consideration, only impeded the current of energy. From this one can conclude how difficult it is to grasp the law of subtle energies. For instance, the fur of animals, because of its peculiar electrical effect, does not promote the success of an experiment.

344. Patience is a conscious systematic understanding of what is taking place. Patience needs to be cultivated as a promoter of advancement. It is absurd to represent patience as an inner atrophy, on the contrary, the process of patience is intensity. Thus energy takes part in events, contributing to them and not making erroneous premises in advance.

Thus one should accustom students to patience in its true meaning.

345. People attempt to understand the path of patience as an undergoing of adversities. But such an understanding will be inadequate, because it debases the meaning of energy. The man who knows that it is wiser for him to apply his strength not today but tomorrow will only be one who discriminates the useful path. He is not a sufferer, but one who understands utility. Therefore, it is so important to clarify the meaning of many appellations.

Each word in itself implies a definite mood. But if a designation is not precise, there may result a feeling of grief instead of joy, and vice-versa. Precision is needed throughout the world. Each experiment with psychic energy confirms what the principal considerations are—precision and brevity of thought. They will produce the best results.

346. Observations with the pendulum of life will show the great significance of psychic energy. The simplest means can awaken the most profound perceptions which lie in the depths of the consciousness. Besides, it is especially important to observe the spatial vibration, which acts as a wireless telegraph. Each hour there can be manifested the quality of spatial currents; these describe the condition of entire nations.

Is it not astounding that it has been given to man to know these syntheses of world events, and that he so disregards his own fortune?

347. Aum, in its consonance, reminds of the same energy which secretly transmutes the greatest possibilities in the fire of thought.

348. Frequently, identical attainments are simultaneously manifested in different countries. Research workers, writers, artists, all of a sudden take up the same task. Indeed, it may come from without, but it can also be communicated from a distant co-worker. It can fly through space telepathically and inspire him who is sufficiently attuned, therefore it is useful to jointly carry on observations. Much escapes observation, because people cannot recall the moment when something inspired them, but according to the theme of their labor it is possible to discern the bond between their consciousnesses. For experimentation with psychic energy it is very important to investigate such similar consciousnesses.

Thought with particular ease can fertilize analogous consciousnesses. The radiations of such consciousnesses will be of one color, but sendings from a deeper tone will usually receive access to a lighter tone. This does not mean that the lighter shade is weaker or worse, but the intense color penetrates more readily into the less deep strata, while the light shade dissolves more quickly in the deep, and cannot evoke the quiver of radiation. This tremor of the aura is the gateway into the consciousness.

Let us not confuse this tremor of the aura with the quivering caused by a blow against it. From the first is born inspiration, from the second, a shock.

349. Experiments with psychic energy inspire joy. Each observation evokes the possibility of the next striving. The number of conjectures and comparisons is countless. By such a path, from everyday routine to the distant worlds, it is possible to make tests of psychic energy.

350. Experiments upon psychic energy are always fatiguing. One should not evoke such tension for longer than a half hour, lest the health suffer. But brief exercise accompanied by taking down notes is useful, because each discipline is only strengthening.

351. Exercising the energy is useful; each testing awakens in it a new quality. It is especially necessary to keep this in mind, for not so long ago I spoke about fatigue under the pressure of the energy. But one should not deduce from the possibility of fatigue that experiments are undesirable. It is possible to exercise the energy without falling into a state of weariness. It also needs exercising as does all that exists. Through rational exercise fatigue is diminished. Each energy must be tested in action. Even muscles must be exercised; thus people can continually awaken forces dormant in themselves. One should understand such an awakening as the duty of man before the higher worlds. The reasons are many why energies can remain in a somnolent state. They can be enumerated beginning with karmic effects. But usually people's consciousness slumbers through indolence. Such a quality is called the featherbed of evil. The best possibilities are not transformed into life when the gaze is heavy laden with the veil of laziness. One need search for no excuse when body and spirit droop from indolence.

It was once enjoined that laziness is worse than errors.

352. To indolence is attached doubt and self-pity. No energy comes into action through such a poisonous handicap. Doubt corrodes everything. Unsustained efforts and self-pity weaken even the strong in spirit. Such an exordium must be given to each one who wishes to bring psychic energy into action.

353. Psychic energy can indicate both the quality of food and the danger of poisoning. Verily, man bears a touchstone within himself. The same energy can also be employed successfully for the diagnosis of diseases. Particularly is it possible to watch over fluctuations of conditions.

354. Physicians frequently observe that a most dangerous sickness suddenly passes off without a trace. Certainly, conjectures will be advanced that the treatment or some other external circumstances have had a salutary influence. But the chief cause—psychic energy—which can produce most unusual effects, will always be forgotten; it alone can alter the course of the sickness.

355. All experiments with psychic energy promote discipline. It is necessary to recognize discipline as the salutary rhythm. The most significant experiments may be cast aside without attention. Something already begun may be interrupted. Any compulsion exerted upon psychic energy is contrary to nature. Let us men-

tion experiments with photographs. If the first picture was not successful, the undisciplined consciousness is disappointed. But where there is disappointment no experiments are possible. Many conditions can interfere with the first attempts. Faint-heartedness whispers that one should not continue the quests. Fear of appearing ridiculous can ruin the most useful observations.

356. Amidst observations upon psychic energy the pendulum of life can provide an extremely remarkable experiment. But for such observations one must have disciplined energy. It is not useful to apply the pendulum of life so long as energy has not entered a state of tension. Even a strong potential energy will not be useful so long as a natural accumulation of it has not taken place. All such experiments concern subtle energies and therefore are extremely sensitive.

The observer himself can gradually adopt many individual details. It need not be thought that multiformity of such details will be a violation of the law, on the contrary, apparent exceptions will form combinations of new particles of energy. From the same instrument two musicians do not draw out identical chords, yet it is difficult to say which is the better performer. Each one reveals his own precious character.

During experiments upon psychic energy, it will be natural to follow individuality of the energy itself. In the wealth of the universe each expression of energy is individual. Thus the quests will be the more remarkable.

357. There exist self-styled invalids who suggest to themselves all the symptoms of disease. But there is a still more dangerous case, when a man has in himself the germs of a disease, and instead of opposing it he gives in to it and deprives himself of the possibility of recovery. In the first case it is possible to act by means of suggestion, for there is no real disease. But in the second it is far more difficult; the man himself hastens the process of disease. He becomes the slave of his sickness and tries with all his strength to aggravate the symptoms of the disease. He constantly observes himself, but not in a desire to recover. He falls into the deepest self-pity and thus drives away every possibility of suggestion. The man is even offended and angry when spoken to about the possibility of recovery. Thus he can reach a dangerous degree of depression which cannot be transformed into a rising strength. This acts as a counter-energy; and the man deprives himself of his basic value—striving toward self-perfection.

358. It is not astonishing that at last suggestion is being applied in hospitals. Several centuries have been required to recognize the reality of this energy. Yet the recognition of it is far too limited. Instead of a broad application throughout life, it is being used only in certain surgical operations. But we possess the possibility of also applying the same energy for abnormalities of pulse in nervous inflammations, and in paralysis and skin ailments.

In short, psychic energy can help humanity on all paths.

359. People are unwilling to see the essential nature of what is taking place. But the essence is not changed by personal willingness or denial. No one can say that Armageddon does not lead to a predestined victory. It is amazing to see how long people have failed to understand what has been ordained. It is thus during a fire in a house, when the inhabitants do not wish to believe that such a thing has already happened. The evidence itself is of no help when a man has blindfolded himself.

360. Observe what kind of manifestations are most difficult for people to accept. Among such lawful manifestations, which are especially difficult to perceive, is the timeless speed of thought transmission. Even observations upon the speed of transmission of radio waves do not convince people. They cannot accept the fact that thought does not require time. No one is willing to understand that a mental question can instantly receive a response.

Observe also many other manifestations not accepted by a consciousness unprepared for thinking. According to such negative signs it is possible to formulate an understanding of that which especially ails humanity.

361. The ability to understand what it is that least of all reaches one's listeners provides in itself the best paths for reaching their consciousnesses. But do not let it be known that you can see their condition. Such keenness people will not forgive; they may become enemies.

One has to understand patience in order to return to the same subject from another angle.

362. The significance of certain moral concepts must be examined not only from the spiritual standpoint but also from the scientific. I take for examination the concept of trust—even among primitive peoples the concept of trust was regarded as the basis of communion. In antiquity people already understood that such a concept had a special significance. Only later, through development of hypocrisy, did people begin to assume a false mask, thinking that it is possible to deceive the inner consciousness. But through the development of scientific methods it is possible to verify the value of true trust.

Let us take the conversation of two people. If there

is mutual trust, the radiations will be excellent and will even improve from the combining of energies. Now let us observe if one of the two is a hypocrite, or if they mutually distrust each other, the aura will be repulsive, with black and gray spots. Moreover, the two hypocrites will do mutual harm, and there will be no better hotbed for the germination of their diseases. More than that, space will be infected from such a wrong employment of energy.

Consequently it is not enough to understand trust as an abstract moral concept. Trust should be valued as a salutary means.

363. The manifestation of trust is indispensable for higher communion. Without trust it is better not even to touch upon such subjects, because obscenity will then result instead of inspiration. Lack of trust in actions themselves is like a pestilent ulcer, which is not manifested at once upon the body. Thus, let us be careful with great concepts.

364. Where there is true trust each act of a co-worker is understood as beneficent. If there was a definite action, it is taken to have been necessary. There can be no mistrust where burns the fire of reciprocal feeling. All the other aspects of cooperation may be regarded in the same way.

365. During a thunderstorm the two human extremes may be observed—some will bury themselves in a featherbed from terror, others will run about boldly and be subject to dangerous discharges. In the understanding of the majority of people, absolutely the same thing relates also to the Higher World—some fall into sanctimoniousness, others into sacrilege. But very rarely does man accept the Higher World as a natural and concomitant condition.

People are not brought up in an understanding of

the fundamentals of Existence. The very attainments of science stand aloof and do not promote the transformation of the entire life. It is indispensable to reiterate about the Higher World. It need not be thought that what has been said about it is sufficiently impressed on the hearts of people. New methods could be found in order that the greatness of Existence be unified in the consciousness in infinite understanding.

One has to grow to love these observations in order to strive selflessly in heart without weariness and vulgarity.

366. Many people observe solar eclipses, but they allot no attention to the connection with psychic energy. You, however, have had opportunity to be convinced that psychic energy reacts singularly to a solar eclipse.

Is it not astounding that people do not study their own basic energy? Truly, it must vibrate to every manifestation. Only through an attentive attitude can new qualities be revealed. One should not be satisfied with those observations which have been made in the past. Each period bestows its own subtle observations.

It is cause for rejoicing that people possess such a force, which is able to transform all life. But let us be very careful, for subtle energies require subtle handling. One may be convinced that even the presence of a single object can introduce a special vibration.

367. You were able to observe how much influence currents have on psychic energy. Likewise you could notice how quickly currents change and a completely different tension of psychic energy is affirmed. Such observations should be carefully kept in mind. People do not know how to conform their actions with the spatial currents. They imagine that even the study of the currents of space is some sort of supernatural sorcery. You would be rightly amazed that many sensible people who study psychic manifestations nevertheless remain isolated units who have no influence on the masses.

It is difficult to convince people of their own power, but, none the less, let us by all means reiterate about the remarkable possibilities.

368. It is known that the consequences of each evil action have to be lived through, yet you will be asked, "How does justice react upon the obsessed? Who bears the effect—the obsessed or the obsessor?" Who can distinguish where the will of the obsessor is and where the will pertaining to the obsessed himself?

Obsession takes place only when an access has been opened. Moreover, before obsession takes place, the evil one whispers and prepares the weak spirit. To those inclined to evil appear the entities attracted by them. The karma of the obsessed is a grievous one!

369. The movement of energy is necessary in everything. Let us not confuse physical movement with psychic movement. Indeed, in ancient times people understood that there may be two kinds of gymnastics—psychic and physical. The first will be even more effective than the second, if consciously put into practice.

370. During experiments with psychic energy, one may be amazed at the lightning speed of force during transmission over a distance. People suppose that a prolonged action is always required. When they say that someone has fallen into doubt, they usually presuppose an appreciable time element; but it would be more correct to say that doubt came in a flash. Precisely one such instant leaves an indelible mark.

One should educate oneself in the realization of the qualities of psychic energy. If someone says that he has already read enough about the properties of psychic energy, pity the ignoramus. Of course, nowhere, up to the present, could one acquaint oneself with the study of the actual basis of existence. Observations were isolated, and the observers sometimes even subjected to persecution. Many precious conclusions have not been published and have perished in scattered manuscripts. You act rightly in referring to the acquiring of knowledge with benevolence.

It is necessary to set aside, in their deserved places, the barriers erected by ignorance.

371. Let us meet each movement toward perception amicably. Let us find the strength to renounce personal habits and superstitions. Let us not think that it is easy to overcome atavism, for physical stratifications bear within themselves the prejudices of many ages. But if we firmly realize the weight of such precipitations, then one of the most difficult locks will be opened. The next one also is unlocked when we apprehend why we must apply every action in earthly life. Only by such a path do we approach the third entrance, where we apprehend the treasure of the basic energy entrusted to mankind. Whoever will teach the recognition of it will be a true teacher.

Man does not arrive at an understanding of his power without a Guide. Many different traps are hidden on man's path. Each sheltered manifested viper hopes to conceal from man that which is most precious. As a traveler who has lost his way, he does not know in what element to seek success; yet the treasure is within himself.

The wisdom of all the ages enjoins—"Know thyself!" In this counsel attention is turned to the most secret, which has been ordained to become revealed. The fiery might, called for the time being psychic energy, will give to man the path to future happiness. But let us not hope that people will easily recognize their heritage. They will invent all kinds of arguments in order to bring disrepute upon each discovery of the energy. They will pass over in silence the decreed quality of their advancement, but, none the less, the path is one!

372. The true significance of so-called mediums should be revealed. According to the meaning of the word itself, they are intermediaries between the worlds. But let us not forget that to all people this communion has been given; all men are mediators. Indeed, the unrepeatable multiformity of the Universe gives to each incarnate being his share of communion. But the fact is that the majority of people do not realize their own abilities. On the contrary, under the pressure of ignorance they try to extinguish each manifestation of their own individuality. Therefore, let us apprehend that mediation between the worlds has been given to each man individually in his own measure. How beautiful it is to study such incomparable multiformity!

373. Amidst a variety of data, one should wisely distinguish the source of the communication. In fact, there may be extremely dark manifestations. There is no contradiction in the variety of intermediaries, because, owing to difference in strata, the naturally akin are mutually attracted. The manifestations may be most repellent, but the sole cure will be within ourselves. The consciousness that has reached a state of enlightenment in all purity is able to keep away from conditions such as those of a filthy inn. It is one thing to open a window into darkness, it is quite another to admit the radiance of Light.

Knowledge, warmed by the heart, will reveal to people the beautiful treasure.

374. Always warn against lower psychism, which can lead to obsession. It is no contradiction that energy can be directed to good or to evil. The very same force can serve for construction or for destruction. Only lofty thinking and purity of heart can be a pledge of the good employment of the power. Each one must keep in mind that he has been entrusted to serve for the progress of the world. All this has already been said, but you rightly observe that the ignorant can find a contradiction in it. The bad will augment evil, and the good will serve the Good.

When people are desirous of making objections, they are prepared not to admit the simplest truth. Whither is it possible to direct energy, if will and thought have been directed to evil? Naturally, the power will flow along the dark channel. Whoever wishes the lowest will receive it. Unalterable are the words about obsession, because it represents a danger to the perfecting of life. Furthermore, intermediaries must not be of a low order. Ignorance and malice can attract only conformable responses. Each one must strive only toward the best.

375. Energy can be applied decisively in all cases. It can indicate the degree of magnetization of objects or water. Like a most sensitive apparatus it can instantaneously record the fluctuations of currents at far distances. It can follow the thoughts of each line of a manuscript. It is an index of the quality of radiation. In good hands it is an instrument of good.

It is indeed fortunate that many do not know how to approach the power. Only after improvement of the consciousness is it possible to entrust psychic energy for broad use. Let this good time approach more quickly!

376. To each one something has been given. It is

cause for rejoicing that no one's path intersects the path of his neighbor. The broadened consciousness indicates how multiform are the manifestations of psychic energy, therefore each one who writes about it should tell what he has experienced and observed. One should not generalize sensations, because the manifestations of energy depend upon a great number of conditions.

The chief factor will be purity of thought.

377. The study of the progression of collective energy can demonstrate that unity is not only a moral concept but also a powerful psychic motive force. When We reiterate about unity, We wish to inculcate consciousness of the great force which is found at the disposal of each man. It is impossible to demonstrate to an inexperienced investigator to what an extent collective energy multiplies. For such a manifestation it is necessary to prepare the consciousness. The success of an experiment depends upon the striving of all participants; if even one does not desire to participate whole-heartedly it will be best not to begin the experiment.

In antiquity people already knew about the power of united force. Sometimes single observations were united in general investigations; and thus an entire chain was formed, and each observer placed his hand on the shoulder of the one in front of him. It was possible to see unusual oscillations of energy; intensified force resulted from the concordant striving. Thus, when I speak about unity, I have in mind a real force.

Let all remember who need to remember.

378. In antiquity psychic energy was sometimes called the heart's air. By this, people wished to say that the heart lives by psychic energy. Actually, as man cannot continue to live long without air, so does the heart deprived of psychic energy cease to live.

Many ancient definitives should be re-examined with good will. Long ago people observed the above manifestation which nowadays remains in neglect.

379. The magnetization of water placed near a sleeping man will indicate the secretion of his radiations, and will demonstrate the precipitation of his force upon objects. Such precipitations should be observed most attentively; they can remind about the obligation of man to fill his surroundings with beautiful deposits. Each sleep is not only a lesson for the subtle body but is also a nursery of psychic precipitations.

380. Also indicative are experiments upon diffusion of the force of precipitations. It can be observed that energy evaporates in varying degrees. Certain strong radiations can act incomparably longer, but they will have been sent by pure thinking. Thus, pure thinking is not only a moral concept but also a real multiplication of force. Ability to perceive the significance of moral concepts pertains to the domain of science.

It is inadmissible to light-mindedly divide science into the material and the spiritual, the boundary line is non-existent.

381. Observations should be carried out not only on concordant factors but also upon disjunctive manifestations. Many-sided experimentation is valuable. It is impossible to predetermine at the beginning of an investigation precisely what ingredients will be required for augmenting the effect.

It is possible to invoke the cooperation of the most unexpected objects, for the properties of the subtlest energies cannot be limited. Such an infinitude of possibilities does not at all lessen the scientific value of the experiment. One may apply individual methods and accept such new manifestations courageously.

No one can indicate where the power of man terminates. Besides, not a superman but just the most healthy man can be winged with successful attainment. In each everyday life psychic energy can be studied. No especially costly laboratories are needed in order to cultivate the consciousness.

Each age bears its own tidings to humanity. Psychic energy has a destiny to help mankind amidst problems which it finds otherwise insoluble.

382. Learn to observe patiently what conditions are most favorable for experimentation. There may be cosmic conditions which will favor experiments either with color radiations, or with minerals, or animals. When I speak about iron and nitrogenous minerals, I have in mind an individual significance. One should independently discern where saltpeter or silver nitrate is better. Many combinations may be found which will produce the best results for strengthening psychic energy.

383. It can be observed how the presence of a person in the next room can react upon the current of energy. In fact, such reactions will be diverse. But people do not pay attention to their mood at a given time.

It can be observed that a man may affirm his mood to be the very best, when an apparatus will show irritation or other bad feelings. Not from falsehood will the man be concealing his inner feelings, but usually from failure to know how to distinguish his sensations.

384. Besides investigating psychic energy by the use of color, make tests of it with sound and aroma. It is possible to obtain indicative reactions to music; furthermore, observe both the effect of distance and of the most consonant harmonies. Much is said about the influence of music upon people, but almost no illustrative experiments are carried out. One may observe the influence of music upon people's moods, but that will be commonplace. Indeed, it is assumed that gay music communicates joy, and sorrowful—sadness, but such deductions are insufficient. It may be ascertained what harmony most closely adjoins the psychic energy of man, what symphony can have the strongest quieting or inspiring influence upon people. Different musical compositions need to be used in tests. The very quality of harmonization will give the best indications about the paths of sound and the life of man.

Likewise, it is indispensable to investigate the influence of aromas. It is necessary to approach both fragrant flowers and different compounds, which must stimulate or diminish psychic energy.

Finally, one can combine color, sound, and aroma, and observe the cooperation of all three motive forces.

385. People will finally apprehend what powerful influences surround them. They will realize that their life's routine exerts a great influence upon their destiny; they will learn to consider attentively each object; they will surround themselves with true friends, and guard themselves against destructive influences.

Thus the salutary energy helps in the reconstruction of life.

386. Usually the most important matter is allotted the least attention. But We shall not weary of repeating that which is urgently needed by humanity. Among these apparent repetitions, We affirm the desire for knowledge. People have become too accustomed to the idea that someone will do their thinking for them and that the world is obligated to take care of them. But each one must bring in his own cooperation. Learning how to apply one's own psychic energy means the gradual cultivation of the consciousness.

387. One should see no contradiction in the fact that experiments with psychic energy will bring on fatigue. The ignorant may say, "If this is the basic energy then why should communion with it cause fatigue?" Such objectors do not wish to understand that during experiments the energy is, as it were, condensed, and furthermore, the surrounding conditions are the principal cause of the possibility of fatigue. Abnormality of surrounding conditions spoils many already possible attainments. Therefore I advise to carry on experiments outside of cities, such a condition will help not a little.

Likewise, one should avoid the saturated effects of quarrels and of any irritations. Imperil will be the chief enemy of development of psychic energy. Also harmful is an atmosphere permeated with emanations of foodstuffs. Likewise harmful is the presence of animals. Thus, each one within his own possibilities will eliminate that which is not useful.

388. Psychic energy is most subtle, therefore dealing with it must be subtle and exalted. One should bear firmly in mind that the force of psychic energy is a fiery power. Around fire, manifested and unmanifested, one has to conduct oneself with special caution. One should grow to love such all-pervading energy. It is impossible to carry out an experiment when in doubt or hostile. Long ago a kind, benevolent attitude was already spoken about; by degrees it has been taught how to approach this most important concept.

It is indispensable for assimilating the methods of experiment with psychic energy to know how to dominate one's own thinking. Not only in order to be able to direct it, but also to know how to restrain thought's action.

389. Rarely do people realize at what distances psychic energy can react, but it is time to understand that events of great importance are accomplished on the basis of psychic energy. One may find remarkable examples of personalities, who, consciously or unconsciously, have been manifested as the focal point of great decisions.

Scholars may recognize the fact that experiments with psychic energy will yield most unexpected results. Let us not make the conditions of discovery too easy—that which is easy is not valued.

390. We give out indications about the investigation of psychic energy with extreme caution. In the first place, certain people may utilize such information for evil purposes; in the second, certain persons may carry experiments in relation to their own health too far; in the third, certain ones who lack abilities for such experiments may start calumnies about the impracticality of what has been given out. Let only those devoted to knowledge engage in serious study. Everyone has had occasion to encounter many people who have made a laughingstock of what is most important. Mockery is not only ignorance, it demonstrates baseness of consciousness.

I affirm that psychic energy must be studied with all attentiveness. During discussion about psychic energy there must be no dissension. Every experiment can be repeated with an understanding of the individuality of each case. Indeed, each experiment proceeds under special conditions. This circumstance should be remembered; for there are people who demand mechanical duplication even from the subtlest energy.

The maintaining of individuality and lawfulness is often especially difficult.

391. One may also observe interruptions of the currents. As in aviation one may encounter air pockets, so, too, in the observation of currents, sudden cessations may be noted. In ancient times such manifestations were called the silences of nature. Even in machines, a tremor is noticeable during a change of currents. Indeed, psychic energy especially indicates such changes.

392. It is natural that psychic energy should exhibit good signs on substances useful to people. One need not be astonished at the coincidence of good signs with personal feelings. Our sensations ought to coincide with correct appreciations. If some substance is not readily acceptable to man, it usually proves to be harmful. The reason is not in autosuggestion but in direct straight-knowledge.

It may be observed that we know far more than we imagine. The process of acquiring direct knowledge from the depths of the consciousness will be aided by psychic energy.

Thus, psychic energy may be recognized as a guide in all the domains of knowledge.

393. It has been noted that certain nationalities readily manifest psychic energy. Such countries should be studied. The cause may lie either in characteristics of the people itself or in the influence of nature.

Certain metals may correspond to the constitutional make-up of the local inhabitants; there may be magnetic currents connected with underground waters. Likewise, certain species of trees may increase or retard the action of psychic energy. Oak and pine are good, but aspen, alder, and dwarf elm are rarely of help to the energy. However, such circumstances are of secondary importance.

The chief factor is inherent in man. It is known that even recently important glands were still overlooked. Similarly, even at present, people do not think about psychic energy.

394. Physiology and philosophy in different languages equally avoid speaking about that which is most important. Though numerous conferences are convened, it is especially deplorable to observe the shifty evasions resorted to, in order to avoid expressing that which is most simple and arriving at the simplest solution.

The ability to reason simply and clearly results from the cultivation of the spirit.

395. One should study mental transmission upon the current of psychic energy. One may not perceive the sending in a verbal expression, but it may be reflected in the rhythm of psychic energy. This is not an interruption, as with a change of currents; nevertheless, the glyph of psychic energy is altered by it; perhaps an ellipse is evident instead of a circle, or the circle itself changes diameter, or oscillations may be evinced—thus one may observe the impacts of thought, if the thought be strong enough. The ancient observers had a name for this, such as "the touch of wings," because thought has always been represented as winged.

Many well-thought-out symbols have been left for our interpretation. The study of symbols will provide a conception of the profundity of ancient thinking. Though remains of ancient adaptations are rarely found, such as apparatus, yet in symbols it is possible to see something far more profound than people care to admit. Still, excavations sometimes yield parts of objects which are not understood.

One needs to reflect about the course of ancient thinking. Such research based on material discoveries can lead to remarkable deductions. Even in observing ancient graphic representations, people often endow them with a personally concocted significance. One should be very acute.

396. This question is very important—Are thoughts stratified on objects preserved over a long period? It can be observed that sometimes they are preserved for centuries. Sometimes metal alloys were utilized for the better preservation of such stratifications. Such an attempt merits attention; for it shows how, much more than one may imagine, ancient people were learned. Great have been the extremes in the ways of life, but at its best the ascent of thought has been resplendent.

397. In studying the emanations of the rose, you noticed that merely walking past the blossom had an effect upon its emanations. From this observation alone it may be seen how sensitive plants are, and how strong their reactions to man. There is also another experiment which has considerable significance. If man by his energy can project his influence to the next floor through beams and carpets, then what deductions may be made about public communities!

It is understood that human communion is possible only under conditions of complete good will. Again a moral concept becomes an actual motive force. Thus, psychology is made a most effective science. It is highly indicative of the epoch that even so-called abstract concepts become the motive forces of life.

It may be asked, "Is a new epoch beginning?" Verily it has begun, because the realization of great energies is entering into life, and science is rising to new heights.

398. There are people ignorant enough to deny the utility of the higher energies. They attain such a degree of blasphemy that they affirm recognition of energy to be an insidious evil. Certainly you will encounter absurd opinions about the evil origin of science. Even nowadays there are ignoramuses who rebel against the good of mankind. But pay no attention to these voices of darkness—they will always exist. Blasphemy, mockery, and slander are the sole weapons of darkness. Yet you already observe the beautiful energy, and no slander will distress you.

399. The signs of the New Epoch are multiplying. They do not perish in the conflict. The flowers in the meadows do not die from the thunderstorm, and the rain only brings out their freshness. Thus, the significance of the impact of polarities should be understood.

400. Each physical touch contains in itself an act of great intensity. Each animal tamer knows the force of contact. Even the gardener knows the significance of physical care for plants, but people among themselves refuse to recognize the need of caution in their relations. You have already observed how even the approach of a single man has disrupted completely the rhythm of energy. Since it is not so difficult to obtain indicative results, then how much more should one apply such convincing knowledge.

People do not wish to accept the law of communal life. One may repeat countless times about the good of unity, yet few are they who ponder over the reasons for such insistence.

401. Few have ascertained the significance of magnetic passes. Such a manifestation must be inseparable from psychic energy; otherwise there would result the monstrous supposition that suggestion, magnetism, clairaudience, clairvoyance, and all the other psychic manifestations are isolated and that they emanate from different sources.

It is time to understand the unity of the basic energy. Each experiment shows multiformity, but within the unity of the fundamental energy.

402. Perception of an earthquake at a distance resembles the sensing of thought at a distance. Likewise the energy apprehends and registers each vibration, from the very greatest manifestation to the falling of a rose petal. Psychic energy is vigilant and ready to register the actions of all that exists.

403. In ancient legends it is frequently related how heroes had to pass terrible monsters in order to find the treasure. They were forbidden to feel fear, as otherwise the monsters would rend them. The particular quality of vision of looking without seeing has already been mentioned. But now the manifestation of psychic energy draws near, and one needs especially to know how to control one's own feelings. One has to train them so as to be able to call them into action or consciously restrain them to the point of complete suppression.

Precisely as it has been said, to be able to look without seeing—this is the best example of the mastery of sensation. For experiment with psychic energy one should know how to suppress one's own feelings in order to be free from preconceptions.

404. It has also been said that sometimes it is not easy to force oneself to think, but it is still more difficult to command oneself not to think.

The ability to control thinking depends upon continual exercise; for experimentation such exercise is indispensable. Each day one can discipline oneself not to think of some definite thing. But one should beware of self-delusion lest the command not to think contain a thought within itself.

Complete abstinence from thought and preconception is already a great mental discipline.

405. Observations upon psychic energy depend upon the inner honesty of the observer. He alone can judge as to when he has refrained from anticipation; he can judge as to when he has avoided a desire.

406. One should not extend experimentation for more than an hour; for one may draw excessively upon one's energy, and this will show itself after a certain period of time.

407. "Let me drink the living water which stands close to thy head"—thus was it said in an ancient manuscript.

The latest interpreters have attributed a symbolic meaning to the saying in this way: "living water" denotes the ocean of wisdom; "the head" means the summit of cognition. Whereas, the writing had a medicinal significance. The disciple asked the Teacher to let him drink the magnetized water which had stood by his bedside. Many sayings can be found about the magnetization of water. On ancient images figures can be seen drinking from a vessel or sacred source.

Long ago people already knew about the two methods of magnetizing water. One, magnetization by passes, the other, a natural one, when water was allowed to stand at a bedside. The first was preferred for certain ailments, but the second was considered better for general sustenance of strength. Such water was either drunk or sprinkled over one.

It is said that a certain queen of Palmyra ordered her attendants to pass the night around the basin prepared for her bath. Similarly, the Biblical story about King David shows the value attached to healthful human radiations. In communal life the emanations of radiations should be very attentively harmonized. Psychic energy will help in the selection of co-workers.

408. Magnetization of fabrics is well known. Magnetized clothes or parts of garments have been sent. Magnetization has been effected by the same two methods—either by passes or by wearing such garments. There was an old custom of sending a garment from one's shoulder. The ancient potentates supposed that such gifts increased the devotion of their retainers. There is even a legend that such a custom was taught to one king by a wise anchorite.

409. Magnetization by natural means is preferable; it takes place without any tension or fatigue, and the emanations are stratified bounteously and freely.

You already know how far radiations penetrate. The atmosphere of old houses with antique furniture must be gradually assimilated in order that the accumulated radiations be not harmful.

410. It is possible to observe precipitations of energy on mountain snows and on dew. In ancient times people understood the medicinal quality of dew. It was mentioned in legends that in order to become prophetic one had to walk through the dew for seventy days. And recently hospitals were opened where walking barefoot through the dew was prescribed; plain water was useless because the particular quality of dew was required.

Snow, full of meteoric dust, contains the same curative properties.

411. If you wish to make a present of a book, I advise you to send it after having read it through. In olden times a book which had been read by the giver was highly esteemed. It was understood that in the process of reading a particular force was accumulated upon the book. Thus, observe all the possibilities of interchange of energy.

412. When a man becomes conscious of the force inherent in him, nevertheless he cannot soon apply it expediently. Many unnatural situations will result, but one should deal with them with extreme patience.

The host does not laugh at foreign guests who have an imperfect command of the language; he strives to understand and to help. So, too, in the perception of subtle energies, one should apply one's whole attention. People will attempt to hide or perhaps exaggerate their sensations, but one should not be disparaging even of the very first attempt.

Just now a great progress in consciousness is undoubtedly taking place. Where one might have expected negation, precisely there, possibilities are arising. Let us rejoice at each beginning.

413. Repulsion is unfitting where there is even a slight attraction. The Teaching must spiritualize knowledge and bring moral concepts closer to the existing High Forces. One should not dismiss anything that can recall a forgotten truth.

Not accidentally do I draw examples from legends and national traditions. Each allusion to past knowledge is already a sign of the dignity of man.

414. Some await tidings from above, others apply their ears to the ground. Nothing in the Universe can be disregarded.

One should understand the most proximate gifts of evolution: first—psychic energy; second—the women's movement; third—cooperation. Each of these gifts must be accepted in full measure, not abstractly. We have many times pointed out the power of psychic energy. Now, just as insistently, should the qualities of the next two distinctions of the age be indicated.

415. The Mother of the World! It would seem that in one sounding of these words the meaning of the grandeur of the concept would be made clear, but life shows otherwise.

Poets and singers frequently glorify woman, but governments are unable to recognize simple equality of rights. It will be a shameful page of history which will record that even now equal rights have not yet been established. Woman's upbringing and education are not on a level with man's, and motherhood itself is not protected.

Whoever is first in carrying out such an action of universal import will be proceeding in harmony with evolution.

416. Woman herself must set an example in unity. We know how seldom such harmony is attained. But if the one real motivation be emphasized, then it becomes impossible to remain deaf just by reason of absurd customs. Indeed, many of them have a historical basis, but these obstructions must be destroyed.

By their own hands women of all races and beliefs will help to mold the steps of evolution. There should be no delay!

417. You will encounter two types of opponents of equal rights—one, an admirer of the rule of the harem, who says that age-old customs should not be disturbed; the other, indignant at the past, will demand supremacy for herself in everything. Both will be remote from evolution.

It is impermissible to drag past offenses into the future. It is impermissible also to preserve the ossification of an outworn way of life. It is impermissible to erect obstacles to free cognition. Affirmation of true equality of rights might better be called full rights. The obligations attending the recognition of full equality will liberate life from coarse customs, from foul speech, from falsehood, from dusty routine. But the new evolution must be begun early in life if thoughts about it have not flashed out independently.

One may perceive that at present there are many women who perfectly understand the significance of full rights. They may be relied upon throughout the world.

418. Universally full rights for all humanity should be a sign of the times. Public opinion must imperatively demand justice. Such fullness of rights must be manifested as a natural law in world relationship. Full rights are the most indispensable condition.

People pride themselves on the abolition of slavery, but has it actually been eliminated everywhere? Can the inhabitants of Earth sleep in peace while somewhere human dignity is abased to a beastlike condition? Can people boast of enlightenment when they know that full rights do not exist?

Thus, one should not regard the matter of full rights as having been already justly solved.

419. In establishing full rights it is necessary to avoid making it appear as something extraordinary. It is a natural condition and must be accepted calmly. In spirit one may deplore the fact that such a natural condition was not reached sooner. But it is no cause for proud boasting when something is done which nature itself preordained.

420. Fullness of rights involves full obligation. Lacking such understanding, full rights will change into arbitrariness. Among women can be found that conscientiousness which will provide the quality of evolution.

Without an innate striving for quality it is impossible to acquire the feeling of perfectment.

421. Woman may be judge as well as legal adviser, for injustice will be diminished when tribunals will reject the unkind approach. Such a distinction will transform the whole way of life.

When I say, "You, women, can comprehend cooperation," I thereby wish to evoke the slumbering fires from the depths of your hearts.

422. Cooperation is a sign of the epoch. Much has been written about it, but life demands that this concept be refined. Any calculations will not help to strengthen collaboration. One may be convinced of this by the fact that a single evil will has already upset an entire structure. One must not think it possible to screen the frightful condition by any sort of external obligations. If there be no confidence, then cooperation is changed into a jar of poisonous scorpions. I affirm that realization of psychic energy cements the firm foundation of cooperation. Not an abstract concept but the evidence of energy will yield new thoughts.

423. Each domain of life has become so complicated that cooperation everywhere is required. Not a single branch of labor can be named in which a man can regard himself as an isolated unit. Therefore cooperation becomes, as it were, the science of life. But in order to give it a scientific basis it is necessary to recognize it throughout life. It is impossible to summon people to it as to something abstract. In each school subject the inherent possibility of cooperation should be pointed out precisely.

Each legislation should allot a large place to the cooperative principle. Let each outgrowth of it be protected by sound laws. Life is multiform, and cooperation cannot be conditioned by a single interpretation. Subtle energies play a part in each work, and they must be very carefully shielded by laws. The manifestation of subtle energies enters into diverse human consciousnesses. It is impossible to define the subtle combinations with the crude word.

Thought must be thus cultivated in order to sense the utmost useful application above and beyond conventionality. Some may not comprehend what relationship the cultivation of thinking has to the laws of cooperation, but cooperation is the harmony of humanity.

424. Much opposition will be shown to cooperation. Some, through selfishness, will not wish to accept it altogether; others will make use of it for personal gains, but will deny its existence; a third group will unite the concept of cooperation with the overthrow of all order.

There will be a great number of objections; therefore the implantation of collaboration becomes one of the most difficult tasks. An abyss of atavism will appear; the most absurd examples from outworn ages will be adduced; crimes will be enumerated which were the result of dishonest cooperation. Too often obstacles have been set up and the new conditions of life forgotten. The trend toward infatuation with mechanization can be rationally solved by cooperation.

Besides, cooperation must not be limited only to certain aspects of labor. Cooperation must be accepted as the foundation of Existence. Only through the broadest cooperation is it possible to find the true relationship between the state and national labor. Otherwise the ruinous indebtedness of the state will increase. The solution of such a problem by means of war will be a sign of barbarism. One must think not about the destruction of nations, but about the improvement of the planet!

When psychic energy occupies its due position,

when woman enters as the protectress of culture, when cooperation is made the basis of the structure—then all life will become transformed. Knowledge and creativeness will occupy their manifest position. I say manifest in this sense, that even amid remote ages may be found examples of understanding of the significance of science and art.

Cooperation reveals easy paths toward perfection.

425. The questions of self-perfection and of national health are closely connected. Let us summon woman to one and to the other. Both tasks are in need not so much of governmental as of family enjoinment. One cannot command purity of thought; one cannot even command purity of speech. One cannot command a healthful cleanliness of the home. Only enlightenment affirms sanity of spirit and body.

426. By what earthly words can the fact be expressed that the subtlest energy is manifested in each of man's movements? How to affirm that the same energy also leads worlds into movement? How to affirm that it is also in thought and in action? It is both an impelling and an arresting cause. It does not grade the small and great. Who apprehends where is the First Cause of all that exists? Who, then, can spread knowledge about the great energy throughout the world?

A book could be written about small causes and great effects. Indeed, such a definition is possible only from earthly measurement. But it is instructive to investigate what causes have produced the large effects; one may be amazed at the smallness of the visible causes. Many do not remember at all the petty impulses. Let us see how such unconformity could result. An explanation may be found in karmic causes. Moreover, man differentiates the small from the great with difficulty.

Psychic energy must remind about the presence of the great energy in everything. Thus let us learn to refer cautiously to the small. Learn how to ponder about the great energy.

427. A careful attitude toward all manifestations is a difficult step. One needs to repeat about the observance of keenness in order not to make wrong use of the sacred energy. Many counsels may be found toward such a path. Love, benevolence, pity, and many other qualities are indicated, but it is necessary to affirm them by a realization of the great energy. It is not easy to remember about this in the waves of life.

428. Why is the participation of woman so necessary in experiments with psychic energy? Why is woman's care for flowers so beneficial? Why is woman's touch so curative in cases of illness?

A great number of manifestations can be named wherein precisely woman can lend a special tension of psychic energy. But due attention has not been paid to such special qualities of women. It is rarely understood among physicians why the participation of a woman in operations can be particularly useful. The eternal Feminine Principle has not yet found its just interpretation.

Scientists do not admit that the mere presence of certain people is equal to the strongest apparatus. Experiments are not performed that could note graphically the different reactions which result from different people. Indescribably useful is each experiment with psychic energy.

429. No one should deny that he has something of special significance within him. The application may not have been found, but this does not mean that the possibility is lacking.

430. There is much activity of subterranean fire.

No one pays any attention to the conformity of events with manifestations of nature. This arises not so much from negligence as from not knowing how to connect events with cosmic manifestations. Yet precisely this year can provide indicative manifestations.

431. Cosmic manifestations correspond not only to physical warfare but also to conflict in spirit. The impetus of intensified energy can generate vortices at long distances.

432. It may be asked, "Whence comes fatigue during experiments with psychic energy? Besides the inner tension, is there some external condition?"

This supposition is correct. During the discharge of intensified energy, there is obtained a specific magnet which attracts a special pressure of external spatial energy. Such external pressure contributes to fatigue. But, on the other hand, such a magnet attracts concentrated attention and makes an action convincing. Orators and singers feel fatigue not only by reason of nerve tension but also from the pressure of psychic energy drawn from space. An extremely complex process results—from the one side inspiration and from the other pressure.

433. To all it may be told how indispensable is unity. It has already been pointed out that unity is a real motive force. It has been said that unity is a magnet. It is a healer, health, it is rapid attainment. What is there still to be added?

If what has been said has no effect, it will be useless to say that unity is harmony with Hierarchy. If this indication is not adopted, a concept about Hierarchy can hardly be assimilated. But this will denote a house without a foundation. Each whirlwind will overthrow such a shaky structure. Whence will strength be drawn to withstand the first hurricane?

434. Many historical examples testify to the fact that even very strong people have been paralyzed by the presence of those of lesser energy. Moreover, one can observe that the impeding ones are of two kinds. One type hinders only definite people, the other generally interrupts the currents of psychic energy.

The first kind is comprehensible, because each disharmony violates the freedom of striving of energy, but the second type represents a cosmic manifestation, as it were. There is nothing good in the intersection of currents; one has to possess a considerable negative force in order to intercept even the strongest influences. Such people are called cosmic vampires. Moreover, they do not betray themselves by their external appearance, and they even appear as insignificant creatures.

You should not force your energy if you sense the presence of such a creature.

435. It is unfortunate that in many languages different expressions are employed for the same concept, obscuring the meaning. For example, the word "lying" may be screened by the use of dissimulation, insincerity, treachery, prejudice, fictitiousness and many other expressions, in the root of which lies the very same concept of falsehood. Different degrees may be distinguished, but the basis will be unchanged. The same thing may be said about many concepts which have been violently dismembered in popular representation. Such dismemberment is far from useful, when it is necessary to know how to think about unity.

There are so many names for the very same thing!

436. The mutual exchange of energies is a natural manifestation, but the draining of another's energy without the transmission of one's own is inadmissible. Such a manifestation is just as frequent as are infectious diseases. But to a certain extent it is possible to counteract such violent selfishness. If from childhood people will impress upon themselves the importance of exchange and cooperation, then they will also deal rationally with energy.

Many aspects of vampirism are nothing but ignorant dissoluteness.

437. Much that is inexpressible by words may be supplemented by symbols. Thus, in every symbol there will be the element of the inexpressible. It is possible to perceive the significance of secrecy, but words will be inadequate.

One should refer very attentively to symbols. As secret hieroglyphs they preserve the essence of the great Universe. Ordinarily, people do not know how to pay attention to symbols. People do not like indications, for they consider that they suppress their free will. However, when people are left to themselves, they feel unfortunate and forsaken.

Symbols are as banners to which warriors can rally to learn their orders. Loss of the Banner has been considered the defeat of the army. Likewise, a disregard for symbols can deprive us of a concept inexpressible in words. Furthermore, a symbol is a reminder of the entire Teaching. The secrecy of the symbol is, as it were, a tension of energy.

438. Desperation is bad, but there is another measure of extreme intensity which is necessary for attainment. Externally it can almost be identified with the limit of despair, but in essence they will be opposites. Despair is destructive, but the extreme limit of tension is constructive.

439. Ugly thought cannot generate a beautiful action. When I speak about beauty, I have in mind first of all beauty of thought. Thought has form, which means that beauty of thought must be understood in all respects. For the sake of the Cosmos, man must not think hideously.

You know that in the Subtle World accumulations of ugliness take place. The battle in the Subtle World manifests both achievement and loathsome actions. Frightful are the conditions in the Subtle World when space is being poisoned with black projectiles. If earthly explosions shake the firmament, then how much more destructive are the actions of subtle energies! People think little about this relationship of the earthly to the Subtle World; to speak in earthly language—the consequences of the subtlest energies exceed the earthly influences many thousand times. They are indeed reflected in earthly sensations, but many explain them only as bad weather. At best they are attributed to sunspots or to an eclipse, but further than this humanity does not venture to surmise.

440. Knowledge is above everything. Each one who contributes a particle of knowledge is a benefactor of mankind. Each one who collects the sparks of knowledge will be a bearer of Light. Let us learn to guard each step of scientific cognition. Disdain for science is a plunge into darkness.

Each one has the right to receive access to the Teaching. Read through the work imbued with striving for Truth. The ignorant sow prejudices without even taking the trouble to read a book. The most affirmative book they call negation. Recognition of the Highest Principles is considered the most frightful blasphemy. Verily, prejudice is a poor counsellor! But one must not neglect all the collected knowledge.

Let us not forget to bear gratitude toward those who, by their own lives, inculcate knowledge.

441. A cooperative is not a closed community.

Cooperation based on the law of nature contains within itself the element of infinity. The exchange of work and mutual assistance must not impose conventional limitations. On the contrary, the cooperative opens the doors to all possibilities. Besides, cooperatives are interconnected, and thus a working network will cover the whole world.

No one can predetermine what forms of cooperation may be developed. Institutions founded by cooperatives may be highly diverse and cover the problems of education, of industry, and of rural economy. It is impossible to imagine a single field which could not be vastly improved by the cooperative. One should not prohibit people from gathering together for cooperation in completely new combinations. The cooperative is a bulwark of the state and a nursery for public life. Whence will come public opinion? Whence will be formed the longed for progress? Whence will solitary workers receive help? Surely, cooperation will also teach unity.

442. Much is possible; it is necessary only to fulfill that which has been prescribed. Especially now, when humanity is grasping with its teeth at any support. It cannot be thought that the existence of a few rich individuals is a sign of prosperity of the people as a whole. It is time to abandon the error that a hundred palaces make the state. It is time to understand and to look into the dwellings of the poor; only there is it possible to form an opinion about the true situation of a people.

The time has already come to realize where value is and wherein lies the rampart of development of consciousness.

443. Who, then, are they who do not esteem and love unity? They have never experienced the feeling of steadfastness which is always connected with unity. They do not know valor, which is indissoluble from unity. They have renounced advancement, which is strong in unity. They have not absorbed the joy existing in unity. They have scorned the stronghold of unity. What, then, is left for them? Either to crumple under the hurricane, or to wither under the sun, or to rot in the moldiness of prejudices.

Who, then, are those who disdain unity?

444. The most obvious illustration of Maya and of reality is found in the heavenly bodies. Though such a body may have been destroyed thousands of years ago, its light is still seen on Earth. Who, then, can attempt to define the boundary between the existing and the visionary? We find similar examples also among earthly manifestations.

445. Earthly victors, where is your being, and where is your phantom? Who will define—is it victory or the reflection of distant events? Where is the boundary of reality? Though all figures be amassed, the ciphers of solutions will not be found. Only the subtlest energy can distinguish between life and catalepsy.

But people prefer to live amidst phantoms.

446. There are many touchstones. It is possible to test the consciousness of people by the most fundamental concepts. Tell them—evolution and development, advancement and achievement; and without any apparatus you will perceive how such a call is received. It must be accepted joyously, courageously, and with inspiration; but most often you will note faltering, doubt, and self-pity.

Joy is not born of self-pity, or courage from doubt. Whereas a single word about achievement ought to inspire. A single thought about advancement should multiply forces tenfold. What matter all dragons to him who achieves? He takes no notice of the enraged monsters, because inspiration is a secure shield.

You already know how closely inspiration unites one with the most powerful energies. Each one has experienced at times how fatigue is dispersed by striving. As a child each one knows the possibility of overcoming fatigue, but, in the course of time, the miserable straggler falters in unbelief.

447. You yourselves know how much easier it is to guide striving people. You know that arrows do not strike a person in motion, and that their rotation returns them against the enemy. Many times you have perceived how wings have grown and carried one across space.

Not weariness, nor irritation, nor divided thought lead to advancement.

448. Once a disciple noticed the Teacher conversing with a passing archer. Afterwards the disciple asked in surprise, "What importance could such a conversation have?"

The Teacher replied, "I asked him how he constructed a sound bow and how he hit his target. It is always appropriate to discuss strength, marksmanship, ability."

449. Each man experiences the manifestation of inspiration, but these sparks of lofty elation occur as isolated flashes and do not transform the whole life. But for all that, such states of the spirit are possible even amid trying conditions. Let us imagine such an exalted state as continuous, it will then bestow still higher inspiration. Of course, all existence shall likewise be elevated and Nature herself will resound to this evolution.

People assume that evolution results, or rather should result, over long periods, but this progress can be accelerated in accordance with human desire for it. If people so will, they can advance by the speediest means. All other elements are ready for such development, but people must have the desire for it. They must not kill each inspiration. They must grow to love it as the higher communion.

No invocations of magic are needed for love. Nor is repletion necessary there where is Infinity. With the simplest desire it is possible to strive for advancement. The expansion of thinking will already be an immeasurable joy.

Only side by side with true discoveries is it possible to arrive at incessant inspiration.

450. Remember the advice that the book of the Teaching should lie at the crossroads. Be not tormented as to whence will come the wayfarers, whence will come the friends who have a presentiment of cognition. Be not distressed by those passing by; they may attract someone without knowing it. They may be indignant, and their cries will attract many. But let us not enumerate the inscrutable paths. They cannot be revealed, yet the heart knows them.

451. It is necessary to confirm the fact that the concept of inspiration is inherent in all people. Ordinarily it is attributed only to scholars, poets, musicians, artists, but each one who is concerned about his own consciousness may receive this higher gift.

To people of exalted thinking, such inspiration must not be an infrequent guest but the very basis of their life. It is necessary only to pay heed to these contacts; people usually brush them aside as annoying gnats, and it would seem that man had decided to dispense with the higher energies which have been placed so lavishly at his disposal. I advise you to reflect deeply—What is inspiration?

452. It is necessary to help everywhere and in everything. If obstacles to assistance be encountered through political, national, or social lines, or in religious belief, such obstacles are unworthy of humanity. Help in all its aspects should be extended to the needy. One must not scrutinize the color of hair when danger threatens. One should not interrogate as to religious belief when it is necessary to save from conflagration.

All Teachings point to the necessity of unconditional assistance. Such help may be considered true inspiration. It has been emphasized already, but numerous conventionalities compel one to again affirm the freedom of assistance.

453. Anxiety of heart is inevitable if you know of misfortune in the home of a neighbor. And the open centers can indicate many disturbances near and far—the heart quivers from them. But people often fail to pay attention to heart signs; they are inclined to attribute them to illness. Yet it will be just to remember that the heart beats in unison with all that exists. Cosmic events and national conflagrations are like hammer blows.

People talk about the development of heart ailments. Indeed, the symptoms are increasing, but it is superficial to think only about the nervous tension of the age. Where, then, lies the reason for these disturbances? The condensation of currents provokes psychic energy to new manifestations. But people fail to give the energy paramount significance, and from this result so many perturbations and all sorts of conflicts.

Someone has said, "Do not drive energies to the point of madness." Such a warning is not far from the truth. One can picture to oneself the frenzy of energies, wrongly overstrained, broken and abused. In such chaos is it possible for the heart not to be atremble?

454. Gratitude is a great motive force. No one solicits gratitude, but great is the quality of this power. Gratitude acts as a purifier, and whatever has been purified is already more easily moved. Thus, gratitude is a means of hastening the path.

Some believe that by a transport of gratitude they lower themselves. What ignorance! Gratitude only exalts, purifies; it attracts new energies. Even a machine works better without dust.

455. Let us not anticipate from young scholars a very important investigation regarding the historical names of psychic energy. Unquestionably, among different peoples the presence of this energy was observed long ago. Each age noticed its new qualities and symbolized them in its own way. Some identified psychic energy with light, adding to it the concept of illumination and luminosity; others noted its magnetic nature or its dynamics; the manifestation of its lightning speed was also observed.

Thus at different times people have accumulated considerable data, each one according to his own character. Put together similar observations and you obtain very significant exhibits. Besides, it may be seen that peoples of early times displayed considerable power of observation, possibly even greater than at present. It is necessary to investigate how the properties of great energy have been collected and recorded.

Philosophers, physicists, historians, and students of dialects may gather together for useful research.

456. Collaboration between scholars has become indispensable. A connection between diversified subjects must be found, because the division of many subjects is simply a convention.

457. It is often observed that clairaudience and clairvoyance usually yield fragmentary information.

But it is necessary to recall many principles in order to understand what is taking place. Frequently the fragmentary character results from the earthly point of view. People do not grasp the subtle connection of what has been seen. Perhaps the bond is quite logical, but earthly logic differs from that of the Subtle World.

Also, it should not be forgotten that the Higher World watches over the laws of karma. Very slightly understood is the boundary between that which is permitted and the sacred karma. It is impossible in earthly language to define the gates of karma. It is likewise difficult to indicate how man himself influences his clairaudience. He can stop up his ears with a thousand moods. It is first necessary to broaden the consciousness in order that all channels be clear.

458. Many concepts need clarifying; among them, mysticism must be defined. If it denotes exact knowledge, then this conception may be retained. But if the aim is not knowledge but hazy structures, then the word mysticism should be withdrawn from circulation.

We propose knowledge beneficial for the progress of mankind.

459. The battle is so great that it is impossible to allot time to ordinary occupations. We are on guard, but people fail to understand the extraordinary circumstances. Even those who hear about the conflict still think that nothing special is taking place.

460. It is not easy to convey that in the higher spheres of the Subtle World, the dwellers there are encountered under new attitudes; it is as if the earthly oxide falls away, and true understandings are revealed. It can be seen how the earthly accumulations, which are out of place in the new conditions, fall away. Psychic energy begins to act freely when not constrained by imposed influences; its essence strives toward Truth. Courage affirms the best solutions. In earthly life psychic energy may be similarly liberated to a significant extent. Thus, it is possible to approach the cognition of the Subtle World.

It is impossible to destroy psychic energy, but it is possible to relegate it to such an unworthy position that it may terminate earthly life with an explosion. There is a complete analogy with entire worlds! Therefore when I say—guard the heart and psychic energy, I am giving most essential advice.

Likewise, physicians must learn to instruct their patients as to the essential nature of psychic energy. It is not enough for the physician to give out his own energy, he must also call into action the energy of the patient. In such a manner the expenditure of the precious energy is economized.

461. A drowning man must assist his rescuer. It is inadmissible for a man to become a heavy sack. It is possible by experiment to convince oneself of how much thought itself aids a co-worker. Such experiments may be carried out also with animals. It is one thing for the horseman to mentally encourage his steed, but it is another if terror and anger are in the saddle. It is possible to constantly convince oneself of the extent of thought's action, when transmuted into physical energy.

462. Observe how psychic energy must be allowed a free moment before action. It is necessary to slacken the earthly reins, as it were, in order to permit it to unite with the Primary Source. It is a mistake to suddenly force the energy with earthly sendings. One should give it a path, through consolidation of the bond with the Higher World. It is impossible to exercise command over such a bond. It is impossible to bid

a carrier pigeon fly, one can only release it; it knows whither to fly. Likewise, it is necessary to release psychic energy from the carnate cage; a magnetic bond is immediately established.

Many will talk about concentration, but such a state presupposes tension, whereas release of the energy alone is required; thereupon it begins to act. Not much time is needed for such liberation, a scant second is sufficient to release the energy. Thus, let us first of all release our prisoner. Enough has been related in fairy tales about the powerful invisible entity.

463. We speak about psychic energy as about a powerful motive force. We are not talking about sorcery but about a physical law. We point out the simplest paths to successful progress. We recall what has long been known, but, for all that, the ignorant will relegate Our discourses to the supernatural. They will make use of subtle energies, but they will not wish to acknowledge the psychic energy.

Thus, once more let us repeat that We are speaking about a physical law.

464. Does not the statement about the physical law remind you of how, in their time, the alchemists had to invent unnecessary designations to find a bridge to the consciousness of their compatriots? The consciousness of people has not advanced much since that time.

465. Ectoplasm is the storehouse of psychic energy. Actually, the substance of ectoplasm is midway between the earthly and the subtle being. Psychic energy, which is inherent in all the worlds, has, first of all, a relation to the substance close to the Subtle World. From this it may be seen that ectoplasm should be preserved in purity, the same as psychic energy.

It should be remembered that by giving out ectoplasm for casual comers the medium is subject to great danger. It is inadmissible to place such a valuable substance at the disposal of uninvited visitors. More precious are the higher communions; they do not drain our strength, or rather, they bestow a new current of force. It must be understood that psychic investigations should be carried out prudently. It is inadmissible to drain another's essence.

466. No one should affirm that the manifestation of the force of psychic energy may not be contagious. So-called suggestions take place unconsciously in most cases. One needs to cultivate thinking intensely in order to attain sensitiveness.

Much is said about inspiration. Many times We have repeated about straight-knowledge. It actually reposes in psychic energy, but its spark passes by way of ectoplasm. Such a great substance must be conserved. The ancients have related that a man can exteriorize his double, which can execute rational actions.

467. It is correct to compare the events of the past, in order to discover their logical connection with the present. Such comparisons may provide a rationale for what is taking place, but one must take the facts in their entirety, because people often isolate a single detail for scrutiny. The scientific method is needed in everything. Only thus is it possible to bring closer the spheres of different tension.

468. Let us firmly remember the qualities of psychic energy. When beginning observations upon psychic energy, people frequently forget its basic properties. They complicate even the simplest investigations by their own habits. Instantaneousness is a fundamental quality of psychic energy, but people have been accustomed to suppose that lengthy thought is the strongest. In such a way they lose sight of the fact that time is not needed for thought.

Likewise, they fail to take into consideration that during a prolonged thought a great number of mental sendings of varying degrees are in operation. Amid such prolonged thinking the focal point of the sending is lost. The manifestation of instantaneousness must teach that a short impact of thought will conform to the essential nature of the psychic energy.

But the ability to think briefly needs to be cultivated. Not only brevity but also the force of the thought must be harmonized with the sending of psychic energy.

469. Nothing can be achieved all at once. Long ago it was said that in a single sigh we overcome space, but it is necessary to know how to sigh. It would seem that in a single sigh is expressed the essential nature of psychic energy, but not at once does this correlation impress itself upon one's consciousness. The primitive imagination with extreme ease constructs a Maya of all sorts of visions, but when the consciousness has been broadened, deductions become more cautious.

Many phantoms disperse before the realization of psychic energy.

470. Psychic energy, like the heart, knows no rest. There can be no long interruption in the activity of the heart, just as the outflow of psychic energy is incessant. The heart is not needed in an earthly sense during sojourn in the Higher World, but psychic energy can never interrupt its own current.

Constancy is also a basic quality of the energy. The moving force of the energy is the motion of the spiral lines of the entire Universe. One may see glorious architectonics in the whole harmoniousness of the countless currents of energy.

471. We call psychic energy "eternally growing." It can draw its own growth from out of Infinity. The only indispensable conditions are its realization, and its direction toward good. Without realization, the energy remains captive.

It is asked, "Can such a precious energy possibly be directed to evil?" Any misuse of it leads to destruction. There may be different periods and degrees of such destruction, but ultimate dissolution is inevitable.

472. Since the energy by its very nature is eternally growing, how criminal it is to pervert the current of the basic substance!

473. We also call psychic energy "the bulwark of self-sacrifice." Of its might achievements are born. The feeling of ecstasy cannot be experienced without psychic energy.

You rightly observe that so-called mediums are not those who achieve. But enough has already been said about professional mediums, who are doing only harm to themselves and others.

474. Psychic energy is also called "a magnet," and in such a definition there is much truth. Of course, the law of attraction and repulsion reacts especially upon psychic energy. Without the cooperation of the energy it is impossible to observe positive and negative properties. Therefore, a reminder about the magnet will be extremely goal-fitting when one wishes to emphasize the attraction of psychic energy.

475. We also call the same energy "justice." Since, through the reaction to the energy, it is possible to determine the different qualities of people, it surely will be the path of justice. During experiments with psychic energy one may be convinced that the outward impression conforms but little to the inner condition.

Knowing how to summon psychic energy to his assistance will be the true adornment of the judge.

476. We also call psychic energy "indefatigable." True, the human organism can become wearied from the tension of the energy, but the energy itself is inexhaustible. Such a quality in the energy points to a cosmic source. The energy cannot be exhausted either by age or by illness. It may become silent if it is not summoned to action.

But what capacity there must be in the consciousness of man for him not to restrict the dimensions of the power entrusted to him!

477. We also call the energy "labor." In continuous conscious striving the energy acquires discipline. Awareness of labor is the basis of development of consciousness, that is to say, the beginning of the action of psychic energy. It is a mistake to think that a single tension will already bring the energy into motion.

When I speak of awareness of labor, I mean the illumination bestowed through conscious toil.

478. Since inspiration is connected with psychic energy, then beauty also lies at the same source. Therefore I say that psychic energy is "beauty." Thus one can enumerate all the qualities of the great energy, but as it is combined with all the manifestations of life, then it is correct to call it primary. Therefore, let us so call it.

It is beautiful to feel that such inexhaustible force has been given to each individual. With such a force we can move physical objects. Since the force is inexhaustible, the size of the objects is relative. Today we can move small objects, tomorrow we may move something larger. In this progression lies the success of evolution.

Not long ago people refused to admit that even physical objects could be moved by the secret power of man. But you have seen that it is not an external force which moves the objects but that your energy works just as does the cosmic force.

479. True, it is necessary to understand the univer-

sality of the energy, otherwise the ignorant will attribute it to man only. Again belittlement may take place.

Containment must be stretched so greatly as to sense the Cosmic Breathing both below and above.

480. Each one who speaks to people is like a fisherman casting his net. One needs to cast farther in order to catch nearer. No sooner do you encourage someone than it becomes necessary to watch lest pride overcome him. Nature requires the methods of the middle path.

But neither inspiration nor beauty lie in the middle; it means that the middle, just as equilibrium, affirms but does not lessen the tension of the energy. What we call Nirvana is the same thing. This middle is not a lower vibration, but an equilibrium of higher tension.

481. The tension of psychic energy multiplies the vital capacity. One may be assured that in periods of psychic tension people live longer. This cannot be attributed to diet or to sanitary conditions, for in periods of confusion the conditions of life are very difficult, and the sole cause is contained in the heightened activity of psychic energy.

But one should fully analyze what comprises the tension of psychic energy. If a weak man overworks himself physically, his tension does not lead to the best result. Tension of energy is to be understood first from a psychic standpoint. It must not be forgotten wherein lies the impulse of each action. Thus it can be seen that the increase of energy will produce a physical reflex, but each reflex is only a reflection of the true cause.

482. When a physician prohibits a man who has lost his equilibrium from working mentally, he acts unwisely. There are well-known examples of experienced physicians who, on the contrary, intensified the activity of psychic energy. Indeed, such healers must

possess a considerable store of psychic energy in order to discern the domain of knowledge to which to direct the patient.

Fatigue is harmful, while tension is vitalizing. But the boundary line between these conditions is very intricate. Experienced physicians who refine their own psychic energy can indicate the measure of useful tension.

483. Goats jump about outdoors, but such a measure of tension is not for man. Let the peculiarities of each sport be carefully analyzed. Many such forms of tension do not promote vitality.

Likewise, let so-called educators appraise more subtly the aptitudes of students. The same truth needs to be told to all who intend to distribute work and rewards according to abilities. This procedure is right, but all the more necessary is it to know how to evaluate aptitudes.

It is impossible to judge the quality of energy if the judges themselves know nothing about it.

484. Do not drive any one away if he wishes to study the energy with a purely scientific aim. Only ascertain that the goal should not prove to be pseudo-scientific. A scientific task is based on tolerant acceptance, but the pseudo-scientific is full of negation. Likewise, do not burden investigators with preconceived methods. Each investigator has the right to his own path. Even if his path be a complicated one, he may discover an unexpected new detail. Poor is the method of pedagogues who ridicule each attempt at an original solution of a problem. Quests of new approaches to truth should be welcomed. If one's conviction is steadfast that Truth is one, there can be no fear that some other truth will be found.

One should manifest the broadest tolerance, only thus is it possible to build up cooperation.

485. During conversation one should become convinced of another's error only after careful consideration. Especially observant must one be of the forms of expression. Often people are speaking about one and the same thing, using completely different expressions; just as, on the contrary, people are able to speak in the very same words while attaching to them different meanings.

When discussing higher subjects it is particularly necessary to manifest caution in order to avoid misunderstandings.

486. Of all that takes place, you should ask yourself, "Why is it happening precisely in this form and not in another? Why just now and not before?" Many thoughts will arise around each event. Thinking will be directed to many causes, and by and by much will become clear.

487. Let us leave to the decision of true science the beclouded discussions about apparitions, forebodings, and suggestions. Let us not be afraid to leave to scholars the investigation of all manifestations in the light of severe scientific study. But let such study be actually strict, that is to say, just. Only this condition is necessary, when we are touching cosmic laws.

Let the transmission of thought at a distance be compared with the radio. Let us apply to visions the principles of television. Let us recall the newest discoveries, they will help in the question of psychic energy. Let us not be afraid to compare visions with scientific discoveries. Of course, not for the sake of sacrilege or self-conceit can one draw comparisons from all the domains of nature. Let physics confirm the very highest psychic manifestations.

Since psychic energy is an energy, it will not contradict the laws of physics.

488. Endeavor by all means to extend good will and containment. Not one affirmation of science may be found which you cannot accept; in such a manner the advantage will be on your side. You will have no grounds for irritation, because you admit any scientific consideration whatever. Sometimes you will regret a form of expression, but the essence will find a place in your consciousness. Such admittance will create a distinct advantage.

489. Wherein is Guidance? Precisely in the indications of what is most needed and in protection against what is most dangerous. One needs to reflect what the word itself means. Usually people place upon it their own interpretation; in this will be the germ of mistrust, that is, the inception of dissolution. The scientist cannot carry on an experiment by premising unbelief. It can be observed that the likelihood of success in such an experiment is three-fourths lost.

Let us ponder upon Guidance.

490. In everything there is movement, just so does Guidance vibrate. The higher qualities of Guidance are responsiveness, keen-sightedness, and containment. Poor is the Guide who is fixed upon one command! Higher Guidance is both invisible and inaudible. It is a special science to give not less nor more, taking into consideration the planetary conditions.

Do not be astonished that frequently those who are being guided do not generally recognize the Guidance. Verily, the Guide is not vexed by this. The swimming teacher supports his pupils at first and encourages them, whispering, "You are floating by yourself." It is thus in all fields. It would not be wise for the Guide to enumerate all cosmic and karmic conditions. Such accumulations would only frighten and suppress energy.

Complex is the contact of world events: karma of races and ethnic groups; karma of personality; karma, carnate and subtle; karma of long ago and the present—they all form complicated knots. To alter karma is difficult, but for all that, it is possible to regulate it to a certain degree; in this respect Guidance is extremely necessary.

One must not understand Guidance as something beyond the clouds; in a different degree Guidance takes place also in the carnate world. Therefore since olden times the ordained concept of the Guru was extremely significant; reverence and devotion and love live around this concept. The living current of psychic energy works in such combinations of Teacher with disciple.

Guidance is a many-stringed harp!

491. Frequently you hear absurd tales of how there occur simultaneous incarnations of one and the same person—a conclusion both ignorant and harmful. Deniers of incarnation make use of such fictions to dispute the possibility of reincarnation. Besides, they forget the reason—which somewhat lessens the guilt—namely imaginative invention. Certain people remember the details of a definite epoch; when they dream of being a well-known person, their remembrance of the dream molds the imagining of an incarnation. The resulting error is in the person, but not in the epoch. A child imagines himself a field marshal, and such a representation already sinks into his Chalice.

Many remember their past lives, but through obscuration of consciousness they call forth their own past imaginings. One needs to be careful also not to censure too greatly the mistakes of others. Aside from conceit and ignorance, there may be only partial errors without base motive. Indeed, there may also be different forms of obsession and whispering with evil intention, but enough has already been said about obsession.

492. Teacher and disciple are indissoluble. Each Teacher remains also a disciple, for amid Hierarchy he will be a link in the Chain of Eternity. Likewise in the descending line, each disciple will also be a teacher.

It is a mistake to think that certain initiations elevate one to the step of absolute Teachership; only continuous discipline of cognition can be the living source of perfectment. Let us not look for limits in Infinity. Let us not understand cognition as something finite; in this limitation we lose the joy of Be-ness.

493. "It is not I who give, but you who accept." The Guide very rarely says that He gives. Only in the case of necessity will He confirm His pledge and give a manifestation of His "I." Throughout life the Guide says, "Accept." He affirms that a gift through Him proceeds from Hierarchy. One should keep these formulae in mind, for in them is contained the joy of Hierarchy which labors for Good. One must not refer unreasoningly to words; in them is contained the imprint of limitation, as it were. There is no reason for forgetting the salutary bond of Hierarchy! Therefore—"It is not I who give, but you who accept."

494. Life is symbolized by a river or rushing current, but never by a lake or a well. Movement is predicated by life. Movement of all and in everything is the basis of existence. One needs to grow to love motion, not so much the external as the internal.

People do not notice the movement of the heavenly bodies in spite of all their precipitateness. Earth appears immovable to the eye of its inhabitant. Inner movement is also invisible to the earthly eyesight, but the essence of man must realize unceasing movement; only because of it can the heart beat. One should not imagine oneself immovable when the planet provides an example of ceaseless rotation; it exists by means of this motion. Thus, man cannot dwell in immobility. Still the consciousness whispers that a hustling about is only pretended movement. Again we come to the path of rhythm and harmony. Hustle is dissonance, and it can only irritate and dismember accumulations. Only a broadened consciousness understands the boundary line between striving and hustling.

Many, in general, do not understand why there are such subdivisions, but they certainly have not heard the music of the spheres, and they do not know the significance of rhythm.

495. Similarly inexperienced are those who suppose that quietude is possible in nature. The concept of quietude is altogether lacking. Only the beginner poets sing praises about silence, themselves contradicting it. But science has ascertained radio waves which are registered by certain people without apparatus. Psychic energy opens up the inner hearing. Space cannot be silent, it is filled with the sounding of all three worlds. It is full, for there is no void.

Let people remember that silence can be only for the deaf, but even the so-called deaf hear an inner reverberation which can be even more exquisite than the outer.

496. Those born blind undoubtedly see internally but they do not know how to transmit their impressions in words. Their colors are multiform and more subtle, because therein they border upon the Subtle World. One has to observe the expressions on their faces in order to notice the inner emotions.

The deaf and the blind are often good and less irritable, not only by reason of their withdrawal from earthly life but also because of their closeness to the Subtle World.

497. Picture to yourself how an ignoramus approaches a complicated machine. He does not think about the meaning of the apparatus but clutches at the first lever, not realizing the consequences. Exactly comparable is the case of a man who has remembered only one detail of the entire Teaching and is amazed that he does not see the whole effect. Just as careless handling of the machine threatens the ignoramus with ruin, so does a man who disregards the essence of the Teaching find himself in danger.

One person is concerned only about the quality of food; another tries to avoid foul language; another attempts to avoid irritation; a fourth avoids fear; but such useful details are nevertheless separate levers—none by itself will lift the entire weight. One needs to delve by degrees into the synthesis of the Teaching; only the rainbow of the synthesis can bestow advancement. If someone notices that one aspect has taken possession of him, let him diligently repeat also the other parts of the given indications.

We give much in a veiled form and gradually bring realization nearer to people. Let man not be afraid, but draw near until he assimilates the rhythm of the entire mosaic.

Thus, an approach to the synthesis teaches one to make use of all the details.

498. I do not wish to burden you, but I affirm that disharmony of details can break up all construction. One must grow to love each unfolding blossom. Let us not, in our conceit, rearrange the laws of Being.

499. Around the concept of synthesis are many

misunderstandings. Though some admit its usefulness, they consider that synthesis is a little of everything. They vindicate themselves thus—that man cannot know everything in the present stage of development of knowledge. But, then, is synthesis knowing everything? Science with all its branches cannot be assimilated by one person, its meaning must be realized. It can thus be fully assimilated and affirmed in consciousness.

Only an ignoramus can pretend that the meaning of synthesis is incomprehensible to him. The ignoramus easily accepts one mechanical branch and is ready to conceal his narrowness with prejudices about the impossibility of combination.

500. It is necessary to show by historical examples to what an extent this containment and coordination have been signs of breadth and clarity of mind. Soon the machine will enable people to be at leisure a considerable portion of the day. One must ask oneself upon what this free time will be expended.

It should be recognized that a combination of several occupations is inevitable, otherwise one may fall into a stupor. Only broadening of consciousness can help in a sensible apportionment of the day. But the manifestation of expansion of consciousness results from love of cognition and from striving for higher quality.

Synthesis will help us to learn to love the quality of all life.

501. People speak of some particular synthetic character, but such self-justification is wrong. There exists no inherent synthesis without assiduous cultivation of psychic energy. Likewise they insist that the physical sciences impede the development of generalization, yet each one knows of great physicists, astronomers, chemists and mechanicians, who were first of all distinctly synthetic minds. Let us not enumerate them, but it can be said that great science develops great minds.

Much keen-sightedness, untiringness, devotion, has been laid into the foundation of each synthesis. It is understandable that the man who develops the power of observation sees around himself many generalizations and apprehends how much more attractive these broad paths are. Indeed, synthesis is based upon convincingness and attractiveness. Synthesis so broadly encompasses the essence that negation is alien to the synthetic mind. One must not attribute the special gift of synthesis to certain fortunate individuals. One must industriously develop within oneself this precious quality.

502. One should cease attributing to oneself different redeeming qualities. In other words self-pity is harmful. Courage is driven away at each attack of self-pity.

It is not wise to dwell upon that which was unsuccessful in the past. Such calculations are called the well of the past. Far better is the spring of the future. Each one can drink of the living water. One must grow to love the fact that the spirit lives in the future.

503. Aum is the combination of the best vibrations; this means that around such combinations one must learn to be conscious of the best qualities. One should purify one's thinking from all impeding trifles. One should not cultivate a garden of resentments and vexations. Each hour should be regarded as an entry into ordained labor. One must cultivate one's character in order that nothing may impede the renovation of consciousness.

504. One ought to test all useful qualities. It is not

enough to imagine courage, tolerance, devotion, and all that goes to make up the armor of achievement. He is not a fit leader who has not proved fearless in action. Each one can imagine himself brave, but in action it often turns out to the contrary. One needs to oppose oneself to great terror in order to prove to oneself whether or not fear can creep in. When I speak about growth's dependence upon obstacles, I have in mind just such testings in actions.

One should accustom oneself to the fact that each indication is the nearest necessary knowledge. Thus, We have frequently seen self-imagined heroes who began to tremble at the first danger. Likewise We have seen those who wished to be tolerant become fiercely irritated at the first disagreement. We have also known supposedly devoted people who ran away at the first attack. We might enumerate many cases when imagined qualities were non-existent. But We also know of many achievements, when people consciously overcame physical reverses and made of their shortcomings the best adornments. Such discipline of the will is in itself an achievement.

505. Likewise people often imagine themselves industrious, but at the first need of continuous labor they fail in spirit. Long ago it was said, "Be the same in fortune and in misfortune, in success and in failure." People do not usually apply such counsels in life; they think that he who preaches this probably does not follow his own advice. But We know those who do apply these qualities in life. It is possible to name evident examples in earthly existence.

Those should be respected who are capable of continuous labor.

506. The worm of doubt is a very indicative symbol. Actually the worm is similar to a bacillus which decomposes psychic energy and influences even the composition of the blood. In times to come scientists will reveal the psychic and physical peculiarities of the man who falls into doubt. The effects of the disease of doubt are among the most infectious.

From the first years of childhood the best prophylaxis against doubt should be employed. A healthy, rational, inquiring mind does not engender doubt, but any ignorance can be the source of the most ugly doubts. Doubt is primarily ugliness, and finally, it leads to betrayal. The epidemic of betrayal is already a planetary calamity.

Thus out of an insignificant worm grows a most frightful dragon.

507. In experimentation with psychic energy doubt is the greatest obstacle. Free, fearless admittance will provide wings for the experiment. You have observed how thought seeks liberation. You perhaps wish to rivet thought into a definite line, but the essence of psychic energy sends the consciousness into other spheres. Admit such flights also, for the labor of thought is multiform. The concept of divisibility of spirit suggests also divisibility of thought. But there occur circumstances when psychic energy is so tense and thought has been directed to so far a destination that such a condition may appear devoid of thought. Such a feeling arises owing to the change of direction of energy.

508. Knowledge leads to simplicity. People who know each other well are in no need of lengthy and complicated discussions; they prefer to exchange words only as to the essence of things. Beautiful is knowledge that leads to meaning; only a pseudo-science will choke itself with heaped-up things and thus obscure its destination. It is instructive to observe the great number of commentaries which have complicated the simplest fundamental passages in many works. It is possible to base an entire investigation on the study of the involved paths of commentaries. The psychology of commentators, in assimilating local accumulations, often completely loses the fundamental problem. All human relationships have the same fate, when in their hustle and bustle people lose the concept of their own destination.

Psychic energy vainly seeks admission, but the icy hand of narcosis restrains the movement of the lifegiver. Let the manifestation of simplicity help to liberate people from husks.

509. The same simplicity will help to discern where is the Good. You have already heard how words about Good have been called the teaching of evil. You already know that evil ones detest the Good; for to them it will be both cruel and unjust. Evil does not recognize Good. Such a situation is so obvious that it needs no explanation. Yet in each teaching we find very insistent indications about the same thing. Such repetitions prove how continuously a reminder is required that evil does not recognize Good.

510. Each toiler has the right to the improvement of his field of labor. This is not only a right but also an obligation. Each task can be improved. Such creativeness of improvement will be the joy of the worker.

It can be shown that the state must encourage and patronize each improvement of industry. Every form of work can be infinitely improved in its methods. Not only do great inventors have a share in enriching humanity, but each participant in labor through his experience finds new possibilities and adaptations. Such endeavors should not be rejected. They can be unified in successful applications. But the chief good lies in the fact that each one must feel himself to be a true co-worker.

511. Fruitful cooperation contributes to the perception of continuity of labor. Man cannot work at only one and the same thing. But by the deepening of quality and the discovery of new methods there will be a continual renewal of thought.

Only through improvement of quality is it possible to grow to love continuity of labor.

512. One must feel how great is the tension. One must acknowledge that there has never been such a time. Ordinary thoughts should not exist in an extraordinary time. To assimilate this is an approach to the front line of the battle. The manifestation of tension is already great, and it will be no less in the future. One also needs to preserve the consciousness of victory as a strong shield. One has to fill space with victorious thoughts, for in them is ozone and protection.

513. Criminality is increasing; cruelty and violence are increasing. It is necessary to look into the root of such infamous manifestations. Humanity cannot become worse without reasons. But besides cosmic causes, in humanity itself there is cause to feel shaken. It is impossible to deny psychic energy endlessly. Because of cosmic stress, the psychic energy of humanity also increases its pressure. It not only is not recognized but it is even scorned, which causes physical and psychic sicknesses.

It has long been established that criminality is a psychic disease. Sadism, cruelty, and violence likewise result from the same psychic epidemic.

It is impossible to rescue humanity from such scourges if it does not turn its attention to the condition of psychic energy—it is growing in pressure. Similar to firedamp, it presents the danger of an explosion. It remains for us to direct it into the powerful ordained channel, otherwise it will terminate evolution. But such influences upon the primary energy cannot be casual. Throughout the planet scholars and cultural groups must arise, who, linked in cooperation, will occupy themselves with the cultivation of psychic energy. Such a network can produce the bases of scientific discipline.

514. Let us not defer actions for educating man as the bearer of psychic energy. There are many isolated attempts, but what is needed now is, as it were, a cooperative for investigating these energies. Such a useful work should not be limited by conventionalities, because the most unexpected and diverse co-workers can contribute their vital experience.

515. "Love one another"—this commandment was wisely given. Nothing can harmonize psychic energy better than love. All the higher communions have been based on the same feeling and are also beneficent for psychic energy. And light pranayama likewise strengthens the basis of the energy. Thus, people must collect and affirm everything useful for psychic energy. Each one must look after the store of psychic energy. Even a single sigh produces a renewal of forces.

It is highly indicative that psychic energy is renewed first of all by feeling, and not by physical repose. Hence it has been said, "Burden Me heavily when I go into the beautiful garden." Precisely burdening and pressure are the birthplace of strong feelings. If man knows how to judge his feelings, he will select the worthiest of them, and it will be love.

516. It was said long ago, "He who knows how to love has a fiery heart." For strengthening the energy, fiery transport is needed. No form of reasoning pro-

duces that fire which is kindled by a spark of the feeling of love.

When schools of thought shall be built, then also the significance of feelings will be tested. Comparing an evil feeling with a good one, again one discerns how much more enduring good is than evil.

517. It should not be thought that in comparing feelings with energy a debasement of feelings is implied. Some imagine that it is out of place to mention higher communion together with energy. To some, energy is something contained in a machine, but such earthly interpretations are mediocre. One should also come to love the entrusted manifested energy. The entrusted energy is a drop from the Highest Chalice. Thus, without love there is no advancement.

518. Again let us recall why the majority of people must repeatedly read through the books of the Living Indications. Some will say that they knew this long ago, yet they do not practice it; then they will call the Indications visionary and inapplicable on Earth. At the third reading they will find that perhaps somewhere there are people to whom these counsels are useful, and at the fourth repetition they will also think about themselves. Others begin by aspersion of the whole book, then they cast it out of the house; later, as if by accident, they remember about it; and finally, begin to quote entire thoughts from the book.

Highly diverse are the paths of the consciousness, and therefore people need to accustom themselves to assimilate thoughts they hear. It is a pity to observe the needless zigzag of the path arising from egoism, arrogance, and contempt for another's opinion. Thus, people are obliged to read many times that which through heart perception could have been reached more directly and quickly.

519. As intolerable as thistles in a garden, so is evil in life. But if sharp eyes distinguish the pathway of good, it should be protected. Let it be long and narrow. Though it be overgrown in places, guard each seed of good. Though the birds of good do not always sing intelligibly, yet each sound of good is precious.

520. Between radio waves it is sometimes possible to distinguish intruding voices. Of course, those are the voices of some people accidentally caught by the apparatus. So, too, among voices from the Subtle World are heard more and more often the voices of the living. Hostile ignoramuses wish to take advantage of this circumstance in order to deny communications from the Subtle World. But they forget that psychic energy is one and the same everywhere. It cannot be either dead or living, because it is primary. Thought is invincible, and it vibrates in space.

The ignorant deny the Subtle World and thus reject thought. All that exists serves not negation; on the contrary, all confirms the one Truth.

521. Many times the end of the world has been proclaimed, but the planet still exists. The ignorant will again find therein cause to triumph, but they also scoffed on the eve of the fall of Atlantis. Moreover, disastrous collisions more than once have threatened the planet. Sensitive apparatus were able to foresee this circumstance. Even a short time ago the planet escaped collision by an extremely narrow margin.

If people are to be found who have premonitions of distant earthquakes, then it is fully comprehensible that other cosmic vibrations can also be sensed. Let us not judge the reason why many perils are avoided—there are many causes for this. Certain islands are in a very dangerous state, yet the inhabitants will not abandon them. But no one derides scientists who investigate the changing shorelines.

Ignorant criticism should be made with much caution, both in respect to physical researches and in the field of psychic prognosis.

522. It is right to assume that the revelation of one secret does not lessen the importance of the succeeding one. It has been said that each revealed secret is only the gateway to the next one. But it has likewise been said that each secret is thus encircled by a higher wall, the approaches to which are successively more difficult.

Let those who fear know at once the difficulties in store. They should not be enticed by the thought of easy attainment. Once the choice is made, the strong in spirit will come to love the difficult path, for how otherwise will they test themselves?

It is a great mistake to think that all inventions are only to make life pleasant. Each discovery provides only a little window into Infinity, and one glance will determine the nature of a man. Not many love to gaze into Infinity; the majority feel terror at a vision of the endless path. Even on Earth there are few travelers who have understood such forward movement.

523. Moreover, people ought to re-examine verbal concepts. Today it is timely to speak about solemnity, however many will mistakenly understand this beautiful concept. For many, solemnity is festival indolence, an irresponsible walking about and uttering of outworn words. In reality solemnity is an exalted offering of all one's best feelings, it is a tension of all superior energies, a contact with the approaching Gates.

524. People can hardly imagine the influence of spatial currents. Even enlightened scholars do not always render account to themselves of the unceasing

change in the quality of the atmosphere; too great is the obviousness of the surrounding motionlessness. Beyond this conventional obviousness is concealed the reality.

The consciousness of the young should be educated to the fact that around them whirls a continuous vortex; it brings no terror but manifests the power of the subtle energies. An educated man should know enough about the eternal motion and about the non-recurrence of the manifestations. Likewise, he will easily understand the changeability of the currents which fill space.

Man should correlate his moods and sensations with many external causes.

525. Furthermore, man must learn to harken to experienced counsels. Through such collective opinion many fires are engendered. One should not avoid discussions, they form centers for the vortices of currents and the change of energies.

Let the currents change; surely after the depressing ones finer ones will come.

526. A certain ruler came to an anchorite and asked him to explain the fundamentals of life. The hermit began to speak, and during his discourse he gradually poured water into a chalice. The ruler finally noticed the overflowing water and pointed it out to the hermit. In reply the hermit said, "True, therefore the next time provide a chalice of greater capacity." By such tales people have tried to impress on the consciousness the fact that beyond the capacity of reception wisdom is poured out to no purpose. But the same story has also its encouraging suggestion—each time it is possible to provide a larger chalice.

527. Why is it so difficult to realize as law, that each energy in itself is also a physical power? People

can move their muscles at will, which means that this energy is manifested as a physical lever. The same thing is seen in the comparison of physically trained athletes with Hatha Yogis, who, to a noteworthy degree, acquire by will mastery of different muscular feats.

Thus, the thinking man often conserves his physical strength.

528. Dejection is nothing but dissoluteness. Put a melancholy man in a sufficient extremity of danger, and he will be obliged to take courage; but the degree of shock must be great in order to force the man to alter his frame of mind. Certain illnesses are even treated by means of shock. Fear of death appears to exceed all human weaknesses, but even such a degree can find something which surpasses it. There are many tales of how the mortally sick received help, thanks to danger alone; how, many times, a paralyzed person has rushed out of a burning house; how, many times, internal affections have been cured, because the center of attention was turned in another direction.

It is asked whether, if people would realize the surrounding danger, they would be cured of one of the most dangerous diseases—dissoluteness.

529. It has been rightly observed that the basic qualities of consciousness have remained almost unchanged over a period of thousands of years. Perhaps such a shocking event as the destruction of Atlantis did produce a certain renovation of consciousness, but for this the magnitude of the shock must be tremendous.

530. Pain is a sign of disturbance of an organ, in other words, the messenger of a disease. But there may be also another form of pain. It may proceed from the perfecting of one organ at the expense of another. Especially is this to be observed during heart pains.

The heart may be healthy, but so sensitive that it is constricted, as it were, by the other organs.

Usually people consider an organism healthy which feels no pain, but such a definition is primitive. The most healthy heart may ache, because too much is reflected upon it.

It is necessary for physicians clearly to distinguish the causes of pains. The realization of psychic energy will help them.

531. Discernment of the qualities of spatial currents is the first guaranty of the higher state of the heart. It is impossible to command the heart to feel when it is not yet in a state to do so; only the invoked psychic energy will provide the impulse of sensitiveness.

532. A special damage against the broadening of consciousness is committed by the man who opposes spirit to matter. Indeed, one may often hear that matter is the condensation of spirit. Such a definition is easy to listen to; but, besides the essence, the coarse evidence stands firmly upon the ancient division. It is not easy for an obscured imagination to visualize all the states of spirit. It may be recalled how a certain savage bruised a friend with a stone and then asked pardon, because he thought that a piece of spirit would not cause pain.

The ascertainment of the states of spirit should strengthen science. And science must help to clarify the human imagination.

533. Each conventional subdivision inflicts damage upon the principle of unity. Realization of the primary force helps to liberate one from unnecessary accumulations. Most conventional terms have arisen from the egoism of individuals, each desiring to name an object in his own way. True, the mixture of languages also has produced extraordinary definitions.

One should concern oneself with the crystallization of clear unifying definitions.

534. About what should one be concerned—the narrow or the broad, the brief or the lengthy? The simplest, most sagacious answer will be, "Let that which is best be lengthy."

Let us compare earthly life with the superearthly sojourn. With few exceptions existence in the Subtle World is incomparably longer. This means that we must be prepared, not for brief respites, but we must especially value that which is necessary for a lengthy sojourn. The primary energy, thought, consciousness, imagination, and inspiration constitute our imponderable possession.

535. It may be understood why comparatively little was said about reincarnations in the ancient Teachings. On the one hand, enough was known about them; on the other, it would not have been useful to direct attention to the past. Only people with especially broadened consciousnesses can delve into the past without harm to their advancement. For a small consciousness, a glance backwards may be ruinous. People must be in a state of continual preparation for the future. Only in such a state of consciousness can they harmonize earthly life. Even in moving into a better apartment people select their best possessions, and no one takes his dirty rags with him. Just as carefully and worthily must man prepare for his dwelling in the Subtle World.

536. In hot weather people on Earth move to the mountains. Similarly, man can ascend the heights and make this ascent with extreme joy. Refined psychic energy helps to familiarize him with the new surroundings. It also attracts the best Guides. It is called Magnet, Bridge, Gates, and Treasure, by all the best names, in order that man may be impressed with his own true treasure.

537. Only a clear realization of the Subtle World enables people to recognize earthly property without hypocritical renunciations. Man will understand what property belongs to him, and earthly things will find their due place in the long human existence. The essence is not in renunciation, but in realization of the especially Beautiful.

538. The man who realizes within himself the presence of psychic energy can observe it also in others. It has been said that cognition of one's own self is the Path. But the first quality will be the state of psychic energy.

For many people discussions about psychic energy will seemingly be a state of delirium; they cannot generally understand what this is all about. They will rage in anger at any one present who attempts a conversation beyond them. It should be understood that the first glimpse of the energy is the most difficult. It is necessary only to consider calmly an ignorant lack of understanding. Thus many cannot at all imagine a state following the cessation of earthly existence. Among such people there may be atheists and churchmen, but they will be equally remote from the recognition of primary energy.

It is quite instructive to note how even the most antithetical convictions can be equally erroneous.

539. One can compare slumberers with deniers. Verily, it is useless to speak to a sound sleeper!

540. Now you can the better understand why Hatha Yoga has not been indicated by Us. Less than the others does it direct man to the primary energy. True, through the perfecting of muscular control and will power, it slowly advances a man, but the most

basic factor with which one ought to begin remains neglected.

Why proceed only from below when the best gifts come from Above? Will not cognition of the most basic energy constitute the most speedy advancement? Not a Hatha Yogi said, "The world is thought."

541. During thought transmissions it is necessary to keep in mind certain qualities of the energy. First of all, one should recognize the inevitable unexpectedness of the reply. This quality is the result of difference in earthly and subtle perception; subtle energies unfailingly encounter earthly conditions. Each earthly obstacle, like a shroud, closes the access. Though this be momentary, yet for all that, the possibility of unexpectedness is already created. People have been accustomed to measure by earthly scales, and they themselves can reject the subtle sending.

Therefore it is so important to cultivate one's own subtle energy.

542. And it is indispensable to remember another circumstance—the heart will inevitably register sendings. This is not a heart disease, but the palpitation of the current. It is impossible to define in words the heart's sensations. Only people accustomed to thought transmissions can understand wherein lies this palpitation.

543. There may even be painful sensations in the nerve centers. It should be understood that such sensitive centers necessarily react to the external currents. The manifestations of such pains are often called neuralgia, but the causes are not understood. Ordinarily the cause is sought in a cold or in overfatigue, but the external psychic causes are not taken into consideration.

544. It is not at all easy to be the Mother of Agni

Yoga. Only in the course of time will people appreciate all the self-sacrifice which is indispensable for proclaiming the fiery might.

545. One needs to be attentive to all manifestations which take place during cosmic tensions. Much is noted, but still more remains neglected. People have so withdrawn themselves from realization of the primary energy that they are unable to find words for the obvious manifestations and events. Indeed, it is impossible to separate events from psychic manifestations.

546. Even the most experienced receiver of thought knows to what extent separate words are dislodged by extraneous intrusions. One can easily picture how many currents are intersected in space! A great number of instructive experiments can be carried out, not only in direct transmission of thought but also in investigating cross-current influences.

Many currents may be sent and received directly. But besides them, extraneous waves may intrude, equal in force and quality—such complex waves need to be studied.

Through such observations it is made manifest that a strong current becomes a kind of magnet for a weaker one, hence the confluence of several waves. A sensitive receiver will sense the oscillation of the complicated vibrations.

547. Likewise, it is clearly apparent that certain waves strike upon the aura painfully. Such blows can arise out of disharmony of sendings and from complexity of waves.

Soundings within the ears have also been evident. Apart from the labor of certain glands, it should be understood that such tension can be evoked by atmospheric pressure—a certain echo of the full sounding of the spheres.

548. It is rightly judged that contemporary teachings of Yoga devote much attention to man's moods. It would seem that this statement is known and intelligible to all, but reality shows that people do not understand the significance of enthusiasm or dark depression.

Let scholars investigate thought transmission under the most diverse conditions. Apart from psychic states, conditions of temperature can also be studied. High temperature results in augmented receptivity.

Of course I am speaking about heightened temperature of the organism. Not illness itself, but the combination of fiery waves weaves the thread of connection and reaction.

549. What thought reaches best? Old people say—that which is from the heart. Such a simple definition is correct. Indeed, the state of psychic energy either attracts or repels the reception of thought. But one should picture to oneself how many unreceived thoughts remain in space! Since thought is energy and does not decompose, then how responsible is mankind for its every thought!

It is possible to verify the sum total of all the thoughts simultaneously flying through the world. It is instructive to learn what humanity is thinking of each minute. The result will be utterly unexpected. It is possible to divide thoughts into a few categories; only a very small number appear to be directed to the Common Good. Such calculations result in the most frightening conclusions.

One need not imagine that mankind has already recognized the value of thought. Do not tire of repeating the fact of the significance of thought and you will of course be accused of an unpardonable innovation, and even of shaking the foundations of society.

How is it possible to assert that concern about thought is dangerous to the state? Yet you have already experienced being accused of introducing something dangerous. But into what a low state must man have fallen that he should consider the mention of thought as a thing unpardonable in the human way of life!

How severely philosophy is ridiculed because it teaches one to think!

550. It is almost impossible to find people who are devoted to the art of thinking. In the simple matter of Olympic Games people are ready to award crowns to the winners. But where is there recognition and encouragement of thought?

One's ears are almost shattered by the applause accorded the jumpers, yet each leap of thought is suspected and ridiculed.

Let the manifested fighters for thought gather together!

551. The entire domain of psychic energy must be investigated by experimental methods. One should not admit personal speculations. The sources of ancient literature should be utilized with the greatest caution. One should bear in mind that many definitions in their time were understood in a way different from the contemporary interpretations. Much of the so-called metaphysical was in its day complete reality.

Many ancient philosophers left behind them only symbolic definitions. They either consciously concealed the actual terms, or, in the usual course of teaching, made use of abbreviated signs.

Deep study of the various epochs of cognition of psychic energy shows the most contradictory opinions. Do not go astray in such labyrinths of human thinking! These manifested errors resulted merely from insufficient scientific experiments. No tales about psychic energy are needed, but humanity will receive a forward impulse from strict experiments verified at different ends of the world. For such authentic verification unity is needed.

552. The mother can lay the first foundations for the investigation of psychic energy; even up to birth of the child, the mother will take note of the whole routine of life and of feeding. The character of the future man is already defined in the mother's womb. Certain peculiarities that predetermine character can already be observed in the desires expressed by the mother herself. However, in this case it is necessary to make honest observations. But the capacity of observation itself needs to be cultivated.

Thus, again We direct attention, not to theories and dogmas, but to experiments and observations.

553. Fatigue is increased by external conditions. Such observations are also needed. The manifestation of depression or weariness can take on an epidemic character. Whole districts, even countries, can prove to be in a zone of tension.

554. Even in infants can be observed the manifestation of psychic energy. But one needs to know how to distinguish these signs in which there are so many echoes of the Subtle World. The manifestation of former lives is already revealed among the childish games and inclinations. It is not discriminating to say that all childish diversions are identical. Even in common games each child manifests his own individuality. Observing children, one can enrich one's own knowledge of psychic energy.

It is a mistake to think that only adults with shaken nerves can serve as objects for observations. Actually, through the undisturbed force of their psychic energy, children will furnish the better experimental possibilities.

555. It happens that medical advices are much spoken about, but, excluding physicians, no one concerns himself with questions connected with the basic energy. Many say that it is not their affair to go deeply into medical problems, but each such remark is harmfully ignorant. Life is for all that lives, and each one must bring his own stone for the construction.

556. From the temple let us go into the cellar. Let us contrive to retain in ourselves not only soaring flight but also compassion. Each man has an open wound. Only psychic energy can point out this pain. Each study of the higher energy teaches open assistance. So, also, the wish to help must be cultivated.

557. Since each man has an open wound, he also has a ruby in his heart called the Holy of Holies. Such a magnet must be guarded. It has been called a precious stone. Long ago the precious stone was spoken of, but then some began to understand this as an abstraction. Now you already know that this is a twofold, not an abstract concept. The nodes of psychic energy can easily be termed a stone, because magnetism in the concept of people is connected with the idea of lodestone. A magnetic mountain is easily comprehensible, but the magnet of man is not understood. Whereas, if there are a multitude of magnetic manifestations in the Macrocosm, then too, in the microcosm of man the same quality is inalienable.

558. People know about the electric eel, but the same discharges in a man seem to them something phenomenal, so extremely difficult is it for the consciousness to absorb the fact that man contains within himself absolutely everything. Such qualities in man ought to stimulate especial cautiousness in him, but

this universal containment in man has not been recognized. The words Macrocosm and microcosm are repeated senselessly, without any inner realization.

559. Is it possible for the great concept of the Holy of Holies to be realized? Sometimes the subtle body returns from its flights with this exclamation, in order to incorporate it in earthly life. Many luminous truths can be brought back by the subtle body on its return. It succeeds in visiting the different spheres, and in conferring with living people in various countries—all this in infiniteness and timelessness.

Then cannot all such qualities in the microcosm make of it an altar of the Higher Might?

560. Certain people strive to obtain only the new, not caring about the assimilation of the preceding. There are many dangers in such leaps into unknown ground. It is not always possible to trust such people. It is doubtful if they can guard what is entrusted to them.

Impetuousness is valuable when it is the result of full consciousness.

561. Aum, as the higher vibration, can resound for the tuning of psychic energy. Each harp must be tuned; so, even more must psychic energy, which is exposed to all the cosmic vibrations, be brought into a tranquil state. In ancient discourses about the primary energy, often precisely Aum contained the epitome of such counsels.

Highly multiform is psychic energy! One may find different vibrations of it that have special names. Let us turn our attention to one lofty aspect of the energy called "protectiveness." It should not be thought that this quality shields only the bearer of such energy. On the contrary, he protects others, liberally sharing his energy. Just as with the divisibility of spirit, psychic energy is apportioned where it can be useful. Such a physician does not know the sufferers who are being cured by him. It is a difficult, but a beneficent task!

562. Vibrational electric massage is useful if the vibrations are concordant. It is unwise to surround a patient with vibrations alien to him. One should first of all study his psychic energy, its quality and tension. Massage is based on rhythm, but rhythm is highly individual. It is possible to rub in completely unsuitable irritations.

Therefore, in medical schools rhythm and vibrations must be studied.

563. The Agni-Puranas, the Upanishads, and other ancient Scriptures, in their basic portions, transmit with absolute exactness the laws of Being. One must not reject but harken very attentively to the sparks of Truth. Two metals cannot be forged together without fire; likewise, a current of the higher energy can only be received by a fiery heart.

Let us not disregard any sources of good. Each one who stains the luminous garment of his neighbor already condemns himself.

564. In different religions there can be noticed a special harmonization of sacred hymns. If one compares the oldest of them, one may observe a striking similarity of tonal structures. Moreover, one can find remarkable common rhythms; all of which indicates that the composers of these psalms had the same understanding of the significance of harmonization. It is impossible to attribute such a basic similarity to simple succession. It may be understood that they have been influenced by One Source. It cannot be doubted that the one primary energy of Existence will produce similar rhythms for one form of inspiration. Verily, the

keen of sight can discover confirmation of the great Unity in a broad way.

565. You have heard that a person suffering with defective speech suddenly was able to deliver a beautiful inspired address. The personal will alone could not achieve this, there was required the participation also of another energy. Someone had sent His Shielding Force. It may be that such a Force will cure the defect forever. It is possible that the nervous spasm may depart forever if the same degree of enthusiasm which filled the speaker when he rendered the beautiful speech can be retained. Let him observe the rhythm of his heart. Let him remember how his successful speech, which so inspired his listeners, was harmonized. To retain the manifested harmony will already be an achievement. Many examples may be cited when the rhythm of psychic energy uplifted a man and helped him surmount all nervous spasms. Many cases may be named when people, under the influence of higher energy, forgot forever their defects.

566. Each excessive strain would counteract harmony. It is necessary that the successful harmony remain in the memory without any compulsion. Anchorites have pointed out the very deep significance of wordless prayer; this was the judgment of those who realized the power of harmony.

567. The radioscope records one side of luminosity; but the same apparatus can confirm the influence of psychic energy upon the degree of light. It can be observed that a different nervous state of the observer will alter the radioactivity. Thus, it can be said that the psychic energy of man and mineral cooperate, being one. The manifestation of joint action or of breakage of current depends upon the so-called mood of the man. Even recently such an affirmation would have been called madness, but now there are certain persons who already understand such collaboration of energy, while others fear to ridicule it—thus knowledge progresses. It is especially necessary to recognize that a good frame of mind is already the halfway mark to success.

568. Let people grow to love tension, for weakening is already dissolution. No one in a weakened state will truly cognize an object. Firmness of spirit has been called armor, but one needs to become accustomed to each suit of armor.

569. Is the fragmentary character of these notes accidental? May it not be that in this mosaic there is contained a rhythm and a special design? Let friends sometimes reflect upon why this system has been selected! Does there not lie in it the particular purpose of reacting on different centers? Perfecting the ability of perception is a very important attainment.

570. The most significant dates may pass unsuspected. The 16th of September may have been sensed by only a few. It is thus when fire is already raging beyond the wall, and the people gather at the theater without realizing that the curtain conceals devastation. The date may be foretold by cosmic conditions, but people pay no attention to the inculcated signs. Similarly, an experienced physician wisely calculates the progression of an illness; but the indicated date arrives and the patient meets the day laughing at the physician; yet how many times has the reply come, "The evening has not yet arrived!"

If people are asked how they picture something of extreme importance, they propound the most ingenious hypotheses, and not one of them touches upon the essence of what is taking place. Such wanderings around the essential nature of things, merely show neglect of the primary energy, which can direct the imagination along the right path.

571. Inwardly man distinctly knows the energy inherent within himself. When he hurts himself, he massages the bruised spot with his hand. When he wishes to attract attention, he stamps his foot; he knows that precisely the extremities emit energy. In stories it is related that sparks flashed from a blow of the hand, and fire radiated on the ground from someone's footsteps. Yet it is difficult for man in his daily routine to recognize his own power.

572. Assimilation of rhythm is a step toward the distant worlds. No one can perceive subtle vibrations if he has not assimilated rhythm and does not understand the significance of harmony. To some it is empty sound, but there are those who have already harmonized their whole life. Not the rhythm of mediocre music but the fiery rhythm of the heart is what I have in mind.

Someone, hearing about the help of rhythm, engaged a drummer to beat into his ears—the dullard merely became more stupid.

573. It is shocking to see the relativeness of people's judgments. Take as an example the definitions of the state of one who has passed into the Subtle World. Of the same person it will be said: he perished, he is annihilated, he suffers, he sleeps, he is resting, he is learning, he ascends, he rejoices—thus each one judges the Subtle World according to his own understanding. But inasmuch as no one has told people about the Subtle World, they have begun to form opinions in accordance with their own imagination; however the imagination is often uncultivated. In this way, the closest sphere still remains within the limits of a phantom world.

When someone weeps at a funeral, there may be found one who deplores such ignorance. Likewise, if someone rejoices at such an occasion, people are indignant at a seeming madman. Thus, people cannot assimilate the relationship of earthly existence to the superearthly state of being. Many cases can be cited when people have seen their near ones of the Subtle World, but even such evidences merely remain listed as phenomena. It is impossible to convince people of the naturalness of the change of existence. They are forbidden to think about reincarnation, and they are agreed that they dwell on the edge of an unknown abyss. Yet each year brings the worlds closer together, and it is possible to increase the number of cases of evidence of memory of former lives. Already each one can cite many examples; all that is needed is an attitude of good will.

574. The same attitude of good will is also needed in experimenting with psychic energy. One should not question it as to the future; nevertheless one will be impressed by the way in which psychic energy itself foresees the most immediate paths. It has been called the "eye of the soul." Thus it has been compared with physical eyesight. If the eye naturally sees the object ahead, then the eye of the soul foresees the future.

575. Not only is each center a dynamo, but each atom is producing energy. Is it possible to consider the investigation of psychic energy unnatural and unscientific? I am speaking to those who have special opportunities for cognizing the energy, yet so often deny that which they already possess. People must learn, learn, and learn. Thus, science in all its magnitude will bestow the possibility of attainments.

576. Psychometry is regarded as the gift of exceptional people, but this common faculty unquestionably

has been given to all. Every man in each contact with objects receives different sensations. The distinction lies in that one person directs his attention to them while another passes them indifferently. One should take account of each sensation.

What riches of life are opened up to those who vibrate to all sensations! It is not difficult to awaken oneself to a diversity of perceptions. Each book, each letter bears in itself a complete aura. Something indescribable, yet evident to the heart, is received from a contact. There is no reason to suppose that only certain fortunate persons possess this gift denied to others. The thought of possibilities is already an opened path.

577. The examiner of psychic energy finds himself in a situation completely different from that of most investigators. The latter can allot a definite time to their studies, whereas the investigator of psychic energy must devote all his time to observation. He never knows when a noteworthy manifestation is taking place. He cannot leave unattended the mental currents, which may start up at any moment. He must know how to awaken in full consciousness. He must pay attention to the auras of people and objects. He must possess patience and good will. He must not complain and yield to a state of depression. Thus, many qualities such as imagination and straight-knowledge are indispensable for the observer.

578. Who can say that he lacks all the necessary conditions? Who can affirm that he will not discover tomorrow what he did not find today?

579. Before cosmic dates there may be the sense of pressure and even painful sensations, therefore We advise developing in oneself the feeling of solemnity. We call this feeling "wings." The rays of achievement

will not shine without solemnity. Affirmation also needs solemnity. Such an entry to the Temple will be most befitting. Let us fill the heart with solemnity.

580. Constant readiness is a quality which needs to be developed. Readiness is not a nervous transport, it is not transitory tension. Readiness is harmony of the centers, always open to perception and reaction. The man who is filled with harmony is always receiving and always giving. His being is always strengthened by an uninterrupted current. There is no giving without receiving. To break such a current is the death of advancement. The all-knowing one will also be all-giving. Let us understand this truth broadly, not setting limits by earthly conditions.

A law exists according to which receiving must not be construed as an accrual of personal property. Realization of such a concept can take place in the heart. No false assurances will deceive the heart. Strengthening of psychic energy produces firmness.

Constant readiness is the product of a healthful psychic energy.

581. An ancient Patriarch called psychic energy a blessing. The contemporary physician calls it health of spirit. With great attention one needs to scrutinize ancient definitions. It would be conceited and ignorant to reject the accumulations of many thousands of years. The investigator must first of all free himself from conceit.

582. A disciple addressed his Teacher, quoting the long list of qualities required for advancement. Sadly he said, "Teacher, I can never possess these qualities." The Teacher asked, "Did you say all?" The disciple continued, "It seems to me that I have not assimilated a single one of these." The Teacher then encouraged him, saying, "There is no great harm in feeling that all the needed qualities have not been acquired by you. It would be far worse if you thought that you possessed them all."

583. A disciple importuned his Teacher with irritation, saying, "I read the Teaching at length, but for all that, I do not know how to begin to apply it." The Teacher replied, "It is evident that you must first of all free yourself from irritation. This murk prevents you from seeing the path."

584. A disciple asked his Teacher, "Tell me, how shall I apply the Teaching in life?" The Teacher advised him, "To begin with, become kinder. Do not consider good as a supernatural gift. Let it be the foundation of your hearth; upon it build your fire, and on such a ground the flame will not be scorching." Thus asked the disciples, and the Teacher was amazed that after all the Teaching a question as to how to begin was necessary.

Not tales but life itself reveals these cases of incommensurateness. The disciple must feel in his heart which quality is nearer to him. "By whatever Paths ye come to Me, I shall meet ye."

585. It may be observed how greatly cosmic currents increase the reactions of different organs. One may perceive, as it were, fluctuations of hearing and sight, discomfort of the solar plexus, tension of ligaments, and ardent burning of the centers. The microcosm is responding to the tempest of the Macrocosm. How much steadfastness one must find within oneself! With what can man overcome the tension of space? Aum, as a sounding of harmony, will be a healing agent.

586. Once again let us encourage all those who are distressed by their first failure in experimentation with psychic energy. Let them remember how many conditions can influence and impede an experiment. Surrounding people and objects, spatial currents, one's own state of health, and finally, thoughts being received from afar—all can either heighten or diminish the results. Many attempts have been cut short at their very inception, because an absurd remark or a hostile thought paralyzed their psychic energy.

It is sad if a man despairs at his first failure. This merely shows that his own psychic energy is in full dissoluteness. Then the investigator must soberly reflect how to cultivate his psychic energy. Apart from experiments, man is not right in keeping the primary energy in a chaotic condition. Let each neophyte-investigator test himself in various circumstances. Only diverse testings can show precisely what properties predominate in the given psychic energy.

Likewise, let the investigator be not worried by a peculiarity of his own energy, in comparing it with the experiments of others. Certain people are inclined to exaggerate, but others through modesty, underestimate; thereby they frequently lose sight of their most valuable qualities. One should be armed with patience and devotion for the observations. One should not yield to unsteadiness and impulsiveness, which so often lead to irritation.

Thus, with continual solicitude support the beginner in observation.

587. There are two kinds of people—the first prefer to exploit the labor of others, while the second like to attain by themselves. Pay attention to the second, among them you find investigators and co-workers. Help them, for such people are especially reticent and impressionable.

New methods of observation ought not to be condemned. Many initial researches have been savagely wrecked by the ignorant. Safeguard the manifested sensitive seekers against the attempts of the hangman. Each one, within his own horizon, can do so much that is useful and unselfish.

Let us be selfless.

588. Even in the most primitive form of shamanism, during prayers, conjurations and ceremonials, the closed hands at the mouth, trumpets and various tubes were used to strengthen and condense sound. Such symbols of tension and concentration may be observed in all ages, in both little things and great, even to the very loftiest prayers. A trumpet sound, in a way, intensifies space, and percussion rhythms facilitate concentration. Indeed, such primitive efforts are not needed where a higher communion is established.

I consider that just now it is necessary to remind one about heart striving. Thus, the ancient anchorites, during mental invocations, projected in imagination a straight endless pathway, along which their thought had to strive. There exist many images that assist concentration. But no one suggests that thought should wander in a labyrinth.

Directness and simplicity will be the most successful bridges.

589. Think not that people know how to imagine. Such creativeness is infrequent. It may seem strange, but an abundance of spectacles does not at all contribute to the development of the imagination, it is quite to the contrary—like impressions sliding along a polished surface.

One is continuously convinced that without heart action nothing external has any significance.

590. Let us manifest solemnity. Let us not add confusion to the tension of space. Let us not exhibit restlessness when it is necessary to foresee actions.

Let us not be covered by a cloud of dust when what is needed is a clear horizon. Let us speak a word of love as a strong shield.

591. Descending into a deep cavern, one prefers to have a bright and even-burning lamp, rather than a smoky sputtering torch. It is the same with the quality of psychic energy. The sparks of a smoky flare do not improve a situation. But how to attain an even light? Only by constant meditation about the basic energy. Like a wordless mental process, in the rhythm of the heart the inextinguishable Light is strengthened.

Let hermits on the one hand and scholars on the other equally evaluate the light of the heart. Luminosity corresponds to a certain degree of tension. Let us see how people often observe this luminosity, yet they find many excuses and denials and bashful silences. As if they were worse than a glowing stump! Frequently, people are capable of recognizing a special feature in a most ordinary object, but they deprive themselves of these possibilities.

If, after reading these writings, people would more attentively observe the manifestations of their own psychic energy, one could call this a success.

592. One must courageously observe both positive and negative manifestations of psychic energy. Sometimes the energy becomes silent, and no willpower can call it forth. An unwise investigator might be disconcerted, but the experienced experimenter sees in this some special circumstance. He waits a while and again carefully continues the experiment. Each fluctuation of the energy also indicates a cosmic manifestation.

593. Think of yourselves not as inhabitants of Earth, but of the Universe. In this way you will assume a greater responsibility. Likewise, you will apprehend how strenuous is the battle for each victory in the realm of Infinity. Do not think that by placing upon yourselves a great responsibility you fall into arrogance. The quality of arrogance befits ignorance. Responsibility is a duty to oneself and to the Highest. Thought about duty will in itself be constructive striving, but for such a path one must cultivate oneself each hour.

He cannot be called a man who does not know how to think about collaborating with the higher energies. How is lofty Communion possible for him if his heart is closed to inspiration!

Learn to understand words in their full significance, otherwise such a lofty concept as inspiration is reduced to an empty sound. As I summon you for the journey, I am anxious that you do not forget, as a result of hustle and bustle, that which is most needed. Frequently, hurried travelers burden themselves with needless things and forget the key to the most necessary coffer.

594. One may ask how much of one's psychic energy can be given away in healing. This is no small question, for the loss of psychic energy is like disarming a warrior. One may give away half his supply, even two-thirds, but three-fourths already places the physician in a dangerous position. In such an exposed state the physician takes the sickness upon himself and may lose his life. Therefore it has been said so firmly about the Golden Path: Everything in proportion, all in harmony—let us remember.

595. Aum, unharmonized, turns into an instrument of destruction. The Highest Communion turns into blasphemy if it be not purified by fire of the heart. Often the concept of the fire of the heart will be called superstition, but let us ask scientists and we shall see that the best of them agree about radiant energies. By no sort of forbiddance can anyone interrupt the path of evolution. The ignorant can create convulsions in cognition, rebellions, and destructions. Precisely by forbiddance the ignorant evoke waves of chaos, but the universal law will overcome all the dark stratagems.

Ignorance must be eradicated.

596. The very same energy participates in the transmission of both earthly thoughts and those from the Subtle World. Coincidence of earthly and subtle communications has disturbed investigators exceedingly; they believed such a relation to be impossible. The principle reason for the misunderstandings is that no one has paid attention to the fact that both kinds of communication have been received under identical conditions and by means of the same energy. Such experimentation must be especially observed, it means the erasure of the boundary line between the worlds.

Should one not listen attentively to everything which can unite the worlds? It is necessary to discover in the midst of life all the tiny flashes that can lead beyond the limits of the carnate world. Foggy hypotheses are not needed when scientific experiments can be formulated, nor confused doubts where a keen eyesight can look directly upon the immutable laws.

Not long ago you considered the logic of certain events. It is proper to observe both external and internal causes. Many do not understand why a thing happens not sooner nor later, for them the most important events remain accidental and are not ever analyzed. But the experienced observer notices the extent to which something is carried out not as a casual matter. Let us observe each manifestation of the law. The energy is one and the law is one.

597. Much is said about trials. It terrifies people that even the worlds are on trial. There is much self-pity about difficult tests. People are even suspicious as to the justice of the very concept of a test. It might help those who fail to understand, to replace the word test with the word verification. Before a bridge every man invariably assures himself of its stability—and by his own movements. For his own sake man tests all his surroundings. He does not like the concept of a test, because it is sent from somewhere else, but his own verification for the sake of his well-being is not repugnant to him. Let him realize that all tests are only for his own good. One should repeat that the concept of the coordination of the worlds is a great test.

598. The individual expressions of psychic energy are innumerable. The energy itself is identical, its basic law is immutable, but at the same time there are no two living beings with an identical expression of it. From such diversity are born many errors. Pedants cannot tolerate multiformity, and therefore in place of a basic unity they substitute conventional divisions, giving them invented names. Through ages there have evolved the most harmful confusions, and few dare to turn again to the fundamentals. Amidst a mass of accumulations picayune thought feels itself even more secure, yet such scraps form nothing but piles of rubbish, and sometime they will have to be cleared away. Sometime the scattered members of Osiris will have to be gathered. Will not Isis collect them?

Humanity already recognizes the subtle energy. People do not know how to study it and apply it to life, yet the concept itself is unquestionably manifested in different fields of science. A multitude of proofs are coming in from all sides. Already quite a few skeptics do not dare to object and ridicule. Not far distant is the time when the unity of the primary energy will be acknowledged. The individuality of the energy will be no obstacle to its study but will delight searching minds. Epidemics of obsession will be arrested by physicians. From fragmentary observations deductions will be drawn and life will receive many conscious ameliorations. Open to those who knock; give help to the sick; set aright the one in error; but be careful with the scratching ones. Especially when you are striving for unity, leave behind every trouble-making thing, for it is not suitable to higher communions.

Protect the co-workers sailing in the same boat, some of them are unaccustomed to distant sailing. Of course, all have not passed the same dates. Whoever has succeeded better also knows magnanimity. He is already experienced in patience, without which no quest is successful.

One who realizes the significance of psychic energy will forever be an investigator. He will always be perfecting himself, that is, he will be freeing himself from old age.

I affirm that psychic energy will not only allow one to investigate it, but its current is strengthened whenever thought strives toward it.

Thought is sometimes represented as an arrow. The impetuousness of the energy is the wings of humanity.

599. Neglect of psychic energy is manifested as the source of many ailments. It can be said that not only bodily and psychic illnesses but obsessions depend entirely upon the state of psychic energy. A man who has lost immunity will also be the one to lose his store of psychic energy. The man who has violated moral equilibrium demonstrates thereby a dissoluteness of his psychic energy. Everyone knows that it is easier not to admit dissoluteness than afterwards to overcome its madness. Everyone understands that the disorder of psychic energy is the birth of many miseries, both for oneself and for others. Man rarely restrains himself, but let him learn by himself to recognize the significance of psychic energy. Let man not be afraid that on the path of cognition he will be left without further sources of knowledge. The magnet of striving will attract the best possibilities to the seeker. Many bear witness as to how they unexpectedly found assistance for further advancement. Only let doubt not overshadow the light of discoveries!

Thus the path has been opened and the traveler is welcome.

600. The symbol of the combination of the higher energies is

AUM.

On the path of labor rhythm is cognized and also the concept of energy.

On the path it is truly possible to realize movement and harmony.

Amid enormous tasks one may discern the sparks of inspiration.

He who labors will be a co-worker.

AGNI YOGA SERIES

Leaves of Morya's Garden I (The Call)	1924
Leaves of Morya's Garden II (Illumination)	1925
New Era Community	1926

Signs of Agni Yoga

Agni Yoga	1929
Infinity I	1930
Infinity II	1930
Hierarchy	1931
Heart	1932
Fiery World I	1933
Fiery World II	1934
Fiery World III	1935
Aum	1936
Brotherhood	1937
Supermundane (in 3 volumes)	1938

Agni Yoga Society
www.agniyoga.org